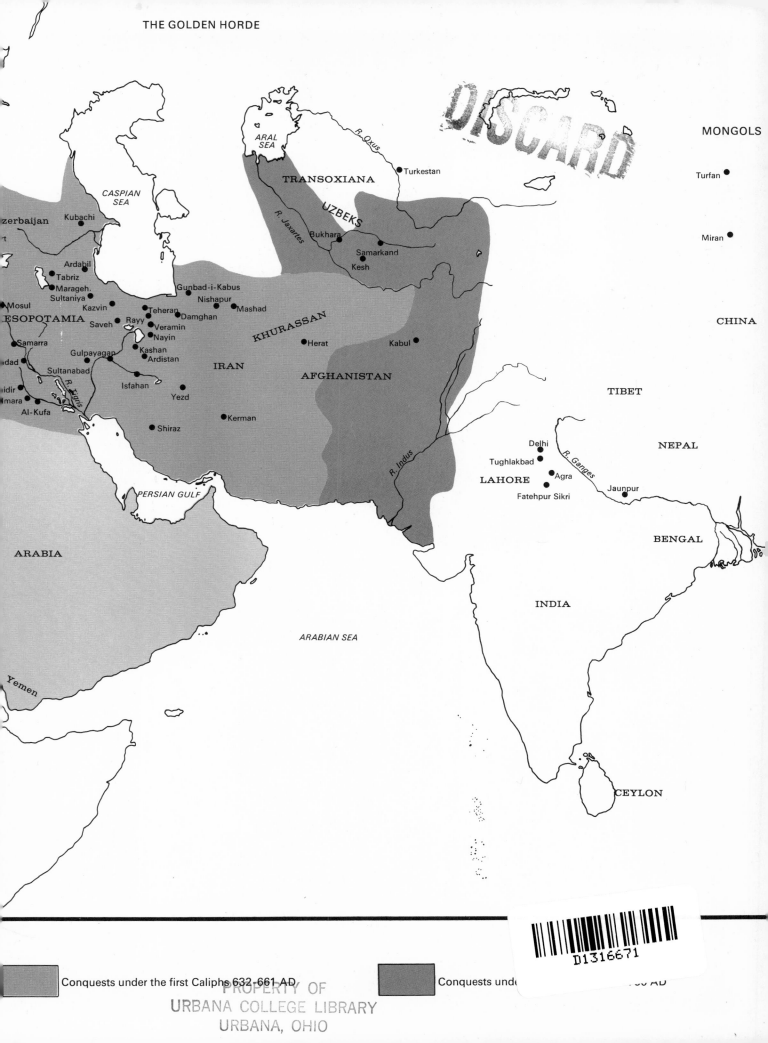

THE GOLDEN HORDE

MONGOLS

ARAL
SEA

R. Oxus

TRANSOXIANA

• Turkestan

Turfan •

CASPIAN
SEA

UZBEKS

R. Jaxartes

zerbaijan • Kubachi

Bukhara

Samarkand

Miran •

• Ardabil

• Kesh

Kash

• Tabriz

• Gunbad-i-Kabus

• Marageh.

• Nishapur

CHINA

Sultaniya

• Kazvin

• Mashad

• Damghan

MOSUL

• Teheran

ESOPOTAMIA

Saveh • Rayy

Damghan

KHURASSAN

• Veramin

• Samarra

• Nayin

• Herat

• Kabul

• Gulpayagan

Kashan

dad

• Ardistan

IRAN

AFGHANISTAN

Sultanabad

• Isfahan

TIBET

idir

R. Tigris

• Yezd

mara

• Al-Kufa

R. Indus

NEPAL

• Kerman

Delhi •

• Shiraz

Tughlakbad •

R. Ganges

LAHORE

• Agra

• Jaunpur

PERSIAN GULF

Fatehpur Sikri

ARABIA

BENGAL

INDIA

ARABIAN SEA

Yemen

CEYLON

Conquests under the first Caliphs 632-661 AD   Conquests und   50 AD

The World of Islam

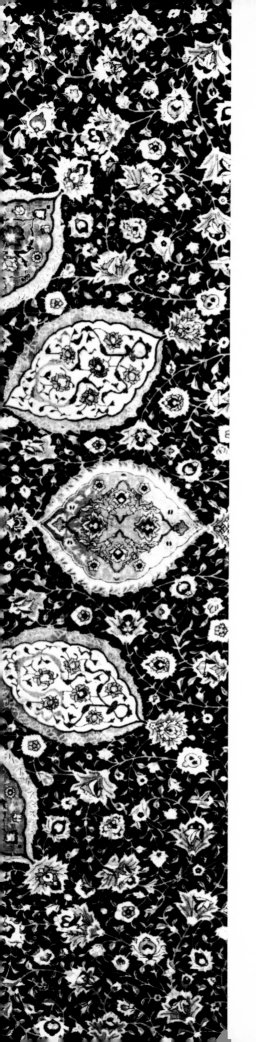

THE WORLD OF ISLAM

ERNST J. GRUBE

Curator, Islamic Department,
Metropolitan Museum of Art, New York

PAUL HAMLYN · LONDON

General Editors

TREWIN COPPLESTONE   BERNARD S. MYERS
London   *New York*

PREHISTORIC AND PRIMITIVE MAN
Dr Andreas Lommel, Director of the Museum of Ethnology, Munich

THE ANCIENT WORLD
Professor Giovanni Garbini, Institute of Near Eastern Studies, University of Rome

THE CLASSICAL WORLD
Dr Donald Strong, Assistant Keeper, Department of Greek and Roman Antiquities, British Museum, London

THE EARLY CHRISTIAN AND BYZANTINE WORLD
Professor Jean Lassus, Institute of Art and Archaeology, University of Paris

THE WORLD OF ISLAM
Dr Ernst J. Grube, Curator, Islamic Department, Metropolitan Museum of Art, New York

THE ORIENTAL WORLD
Jeannine Auboyer, Chief Curator, Musée Guimet, Paris
Dr Roger Goepper, Director of the Museum of Far Eastern Art, Cologne

THE MEDIEVAL WORLD
Peter Kidson, Conway Librarian, Courtauld Institute of Art, London

MAN AND THE RENAISSANCE
Andrew Martindale, Senior Lecturer in the School of Fine Arts, University of East Anglia

THE AGE OF BAROQUE
Michael Kitson, Senior Lecturer in the History of Art, Courtauld Institute of Art, London

THE MODERN WORLD
Norbert Lynton, Head of the School of Art History and General Studies, Chelsea School of Art, London

PUBLISHED BY
PAUL HAMLYN LIMITED · DRURY HOUSE ·
RUSSELL STREET · LONDON · W.C.2
FIRST EDITION 1966
SECOND IMPRESSION 1967
© PAUL HAMLYN LIMITED 1966
PRINTED IN THE NETHERLANDS BY JOH. ENSCHEDÉ EN ZONEN
GRAFISCHE INRICHTING N.V. · HAARLEM

Previous pages: detail of figure 87, page 162

List of Contents

Colour Plates

Opposite: One side of a lacquer bookbinding in the style of Sultan Muhammad. Persia. *c.* 1540. British Museum, London.

Introduction

The numbers in the margins refer to the illustrations: heavy type for colour plates, italics for black and white illustrations. The letters refer to plans A–J.

THE BEGINNINGS OF ISLAM

The religion of Islam, which gave its name to a vast empire, governed from the first every aspect of its civilisation. Significantly enough, its founder, Muhammad, was not only a Prophet. He was also leader, judge, legislator and general, and the caliphs (khalifah) or 'successors' who came after him inherited and assumed all these roles.

Muhammad founded the nucleus of the Muslim empire not by religious conversion alone but by force, political manœuvres and administrative ability. First a caravan leader, then a Meccan tradesman, his ambition became to restore the religion of Abraham and the belief in one God and the future life to a country in which a low form of polytheism was general with some converts to Christianity or Judaism. He first gathered around him a small group of followers at Mecca. As his influence increased, rulers of the Meccan community began to fear his autocracy and resent his denial of their gods and goddesses. Dissension was followed by force and the Muslims were besieged and persecuted. Finally Muhammad accepted the invitation of Yathrib, thereafter known as Medina (the City of the Prophet), to take his refuge there. His famous flight, *(hijra* or *hejira)* in 622, is taken as the date for the initiation of the Muslim era. From Medina Muhammad started a series of armed campaigns against Mecca, securing the right to make pilgrimages there which won important converts. Finally he invaded and took control of Mecca, thenceforth the religious centre of Islam. He had all pagan idols destroyed and sent missives to all known sovereigns and rulers promising them safety only if they were converted to Islam. At the time of his death in 632 he was organising a campaign against Syria.

In the Koran (Quran), the Holy Book of Islam, which embodies all his teachings and in the Hadith (traditions), a collection of his sayings and decisions not recorded in the Koran and often, in fact, apocryphal, a whole system was laid down, covering every aspect of life—religious, social and legal, and on these writings the educational structure and whole administration was based. In this way, Islam (I submit—to the will of Allah) brought in its train a unifying and stabilising force. When East, West and Central Asia were subdued by the relentless campaigns of the Arabs in the late 7th and the 8th centuries, the leaders of the invading armies were given a voice of authority with which to bring political order to a vast area of countries and states.

The period following the death of the Prophet was one of successive victories for the Arab generals. The Arabs had begun by raiding and plundering Palestine and Iraq. Finding victory easy, the Islamic armies rode on and conquered Syria in 636, Mesopotamia in 637, invading Egypt in 639 and entering Alexandria three years later. Having conquered Syria and Egypt, they overwhelmed and converted Persia, took over western Turkestan and part of the Punjab, and seized North Africa and Spain. In less than a century half the known civilised world, from Spain to the borders of China, was in the hands of the Muslims, unified under the new cultural force of Islam.

COMPLEX BLEND OF CULTURES

Islamic art, therefore, is not the art of a particular country or a particular people. It is the art of a civilisation formed by a combination of historical circumstances: the conquest of the Ancient World by the Arabs, the enforced unification of a vast territory under the banner of Islam, a territory which was in turn invaded by various groups of alien peoples. From the start, the direction of Islamic art was largely determined by political structures which cut across geographical and sociological boundaries. For this reason the art of the Islamic world is discussed in this book under the various dynasties who came to power, ruled over and segmented the original Muslim empire. Each section has a brief historical introduction so that gradually the broad lines of development emerge.

The complex nature of Islamic art developed on the basis of pre-Islamic traditions in the various countries conquered and a closely integrated blend of Arab, Turkish and Persian traditions brought together in all parts of the new Muslim empire.

The Arab element is probably at all times the most important. It contributed the basis for the development of Islamic art with the message of Islam, the language of its Holy Book, the Koran, and the Arabic form of writing. This last became the most important single feature of all Islamic art leading to the development of an infinite variety of abstract ornament and an entire system of linear abstraction that is peculiar to all forms of Islamic art and can in all its manifestations in one way or another be traced back to Arabic origins. The Arabs were deeply interested in mathematics and astronomy, furthering the knowledge that they had inherited from the Romans. They applied this knowledge of geometric principles and an innate sense of rhythm (which also characterises their poetry and music) to the formulation of the complex repeat patterns seen in all their decoration.

The Turkish element in Islamic art consists mainly of an indigenous concept of abstraction that the Turkish peoples of Central Asia applied to any culture and art form that they met with on their long journey from 'Innermost Asia' to Egypt. They brought an important tradition of both figurative and non-figurative design from eastern to western Asia, creating an unmistakably Turkish iconography. The importance of the Turkish element in Islamic culture can perhaps best be appreciated if one realises that the larger part of the Islamic world was ruled by Turkish peoples from the 10th to the 19th century. The art of the Islamic world owes a great deal to the rule of these Turkish dynasties, and the influence of Turkish thought, taste and tradition on the art of Islam in general can hardly be overestimated.

The Persian element in Islamic art is perhaps most difficult to define; it seems to consist of a peculiarly lyrical

Chronological Chart of Islamic Dynasties

|600|700|800|900|1000|1100|1200|1300|1400|1500|1600|1700|1800|1900|

● Muhammadan era initiated

ORTHODOX CALIPHS (MECCA)
(period of conquests and rapid expansion)

UMMAYADS
(first caliphate, capital Damascus, Syria)

ABBASIDS
(capital Baghdad, then Samarra; last caliph killed in 1258)

UMMAYADS OF SPAIN
(capital Cordoba, palatial city Madinat-al-Zahra)

SAMANIDS
(art centres Nishapur and Samarkand)

TULUNIDS OF EGYPT
(capital Cairo)

IKHSHIDIDS (EGYPT)

BUYIDS
(area south of Caspian Sea; took control of Baghdad by mid 10th century)

GHAZNAVIDS OF AFGHANISTAN

FATIMIDS OF EGYPT
(also in control of North Africa 900-972, and of Sicily 909-1071)

SELJUK TURKS IN IRAN
(capital Rayy)

ALMORAVIDES AND ALMOHADES
(minor dynasties in Spain and North Africa)

SELJUK TURKS IN ANATOLIA
(capital Konya)

GHORID SULTANS OF INDIA

URTHUKIDS
(Atabeks of Diyar Bakr, Upper Mesopotamia)

ZANGIDS
(seat of court, Damascus, capitals Mosul and Aleppo)

AYYUBIDS IN EGYPT
(dynasty of Saladin)

SLAVE KINGS OF DELHI
(founded by Kutb al-din Aibak)

MONGOLS (ILKHANS)
(capital Tabriz, then Sultaniya)

NASRIDS OF SPAIN
*(Alhambra Palace, Granada; last Muslim rulers of Spain, succeeded by
Ferdinand and Isabella of Castile)*

MAMLUKS (EGYPT *and part of* SYRIA)

KHALJI DYNASTY (INDIA)

OTTOMAN or 'OSMANLI' TURKS
*(Turkey and Asia Minor; capital from 1326 Bursa, from 1453 Istanbul;
in control of Egypt 1517-1805)*

MUZZAFARIDS AND JALAIRIDS
(local governor dynasties, west and south Iran)

TUGHLAK DYNASTY (INDIA)

TiMURIDS
(capital Samarkand, then Herat)

KARA-KUYUNLI TURKOMANS
(Tabriz; took over west and south Iran from Timurids)

SAYYIDS (INDIA)

LODIS (INDIA)

UZBEKS
*(took over from Timurids in Transoxiana, now Uzbekistan,
U.S.S.R.)*

SAFAVIDS OF PERSIA
(Tabriz, Kazwin, Isfahan)

MUGHAL EMPERORS OF INDIA
(Delhi, Fatehpur Sikri, Red Fort, Agra)

*Reference is sometimes made in this book to Muslim dating.
The Islamic era began in 622 AD which corresponds to AH 1 (anno hijra or hejira—
year of the flight of Muhammad to Medina).*

1. **View of Mecca showing the Great Mosque and Kaaba.**
The Kaaba, today in the centre of the Great Mosque, is a plain
cubic building, which is the focal point towards which all
Muslims turn in prayer all over the world. The holiest sanctuary
of Arabia, the Kaaba became the centre of Islam after the
change of the *kibla*, or the direction of prayer, from Jerusalem
to Mecca by the Prophet. It is also the centre of the pilgrimage
(hajj) which is one of the duties of every Muslim.

poetical attitude, a metaphysical tendency which in the
realm of emotional and religious experience leads to an
extraordinary flowering of mysticism. The major schools of
Muslim painting developed in Iran on the basis of Persian
literature. Not only an entire iconography but also a
specific imagery, abstract-poetical in its realisation, was
created in Iran in the later part of the 14th and in the 15th
century that is without parallel in any other part of the
Muslim world. The same attitude that creates in the field of
painting an art form of the greatest beauty but of complete
fantasy and unreality enters into architecture, creating
forms of decoration that seem to negate the very nature of
architecture and the basic principles of weight and stress, of
relief and support, fusing all elements into a unity of fantastic unreality, a floating world of imagination.

Even though these three elements of Islamic culture are
at times clearly definable and separate and each contributes
more or less equally to the development of Islamic art, in
most periods they are so closely interwoven and integrated
that one cannot often clearly distinguish between them.
All the regions of the Muslim world share a great many
fundamental artistic features that draw the whole vast

territory together in a super-national, -ethnic and -geo-
graphical unity which is paralleled in the history of human
culture only by the similar domination of the Ancient
World by Rome.

INFLUENCE OF RELIGION ON CULTURE

Of all elements in Islamic art the most important, undoubtedly, is religion. The multitude of small empires and
kingdoms that had adopted Islam felt—in spite of racial
prides and jealousies—first and foremost Muslim and not
Arab, Turkish, or Persian. They all knew, spoke, and wrote
some Arabic, the language of the Koran. They all assembled in the mosque, the religious building that with minor
alterations was of the same design throughout the Muslim
world, and they all faced Mecca, the centre of Islam, sym-
bolised by the Kaaba (Qaaba), a pre-Muslim sanctuary
adopted by Muhammad as the point towards which each
Muslim should turn in prayer. In every prayer hall there
was a focal or *kibla* wall, which faced Mecca, with a central niche, the *mihrab*. All Muslims shared the basic belief
in Muhammad's message: the recognition of the all-
embracing power and absolute superiority of the One

God (Allah). The creed of all Muslims reads alike: 'There is no god but God (Allah) and Muhammad is his Prophet.' In all Muslims of every race and country there is the same feeling of being equal in the face of Allah on the day of judgment.

The experience of the infinite on the one hand, with the worthlessness of the transient earthly existence of man on the other is known to all Muslims and forms part of all Muslim art. It finds different but basically related expression. The most fundamental is the creation of the infinite pattern that appears in a fully developed form very early on and is a major element of Islamic art at all periods. The infinite continuation of a given pattern, whether abstract, semi-abstract or even partly figurative, is on the one hand the expression of a profound belief in the eternity of all true being and on the other a disregard for temporary existence. In making visible only part of a pattern that exists in its complete form only in infinity, the Islamic artist relates the static, limited, seemingly definite object to infinity itself.

An arabesque design, based on an infinite leaf-scroll pattern that, by division of elements (stem, leaf, blossom) generates new variations of the same original elements, is in itself the perfect application of the principle of Islamic design and can be applied to any given surface, the cover of a small metal box or the glazed curve of a monumental dome. Both the small box and the huge dome of a mosque are regarded in the same way, differing only in form, not in quality. With this possibility of giving equal value to everything that exists or bringing to one level of existence everything within the realm of the visual arts, a basis for a unity of style is provided that transcends the limits of period or country.

One of the most fundamental principles of the Islamic style deriving from the same basic idea is the dissolution of matter. The idea of transformation, therefore, is of the utmost importance. The ornamentation of surfaces of any kind in any medium with the infinite pattern serves the same purpose—to disguise and 'dissolve' the matter, whether it be monumental architecture or a small metal box. The result is a world which is not a reflection of the actual object, but that of the superimposed element that serves to transcend the momentary and limited individual appearance of a work of art drawing it into the greater and solely valid realm of infinite and continuous being.

This idea is emphasised by the way in which architectural decoration is used. Solid walls are disguised behind plaster and tile decoration, vaults and arches are covered with floral and epigraphic ornament that dissolve their structural strength and function, and domes are filled with radiating designs of infinite patterns, bursting suns, or fantastic floating canopies of a multitude of mukkarnas, that banish the solidity of stone and masonry and give them a peculiarly ephemeral quality as if the crystallisation of the design is their only reality.

It is perhaps in this element, which has no true parallel in the history of art, that Islamic art joins in the religious experience of Islam and it is in this sense, and in this sense alone, that it can be called a religious art. Characteristically very little actual, religious iconography in the ordinary sense exists in Islam.

Although a great many fundamental forms and concepts remained more or less stable and unchanged throughout Islamic art—especially in architecture—the variety of individual forms is astonishing and can again be called exceptional. Almost every country at every period created forms of art that have no parallel in another, and the variations on a common theme, that are carried through from one period to another, are even more remarkable.

THE NATURE OF ISLAMIC DECORATION

Apart from the naturalistic, semi-naturalistic and abstract geometrical forms used in the infinite pattern, Arabic calligraphy played a dominant role in Islamic art and was integrated into every sort of decorative scheme. There are two main scripts in Islamic calligraphy: the angular *Kufic* and the cursive *Naskhi*.

Kufic, the earliest form, which is alleged to have been invented at Kufa, south of Baghdad, accentuates the vertical strokes of the characters. It was used extensively during the first five centuries of Islam in architecture, for copies of the Koran, textiles and pottery. There are eight different types of Kufic out of which only three are mentioned here: a) simple Kufic; b) foliated Kufic which appeared in Egypt during the 9th century and has the vertical strokes ending in lobed leaves or half-palmettes; c) floriated Kufic in which floral motifs and scrolls are added to the leaves and half-palmettes. This seems also to have been developed in Egypt during the 9th century and reached its highest development there under the Fatimids (969–1171).

From the 11th century onward, Naskhi gradually replaced Kufic. Though a kind of cursive style was already known in the 7th century AD, the invention of Naskhi is attributed to Ibn Muqla. Ibn Muqla lived in Baghdad during the 10th century and is also responsible for the development of another type of cursive writing: the *thuluth*, or *thulth*. This closely follows Naskhi but certain elements, like vertical strokes or horizontal lines, are exaggerated.

In Iran several cursive styles were invented and developed among which *taliq* was important. Out of taliq developed *nastaliq*, which is a more beautiful, elegant and cursive form of writing. Its inventor was Mir Ali Tabrizi, who was active in the second half of the 14th century. Nastaliq became the predominant style of Persian calligraphy during the 15th and 16th centuries.

Another important aspect of Islamic art, generally completely unknown, is its rich pictorial and iconographical tradition. The misconception that Islam was an iconoclastic, or anti-imagistic culture and that the representation of human beings or living creatures in general was prohibited, is still deeply rooted although the existence of figurative painting in Iran has been recognised now for almost half a century. There is no prohibition against the painting of

2a). **Simple Kufic** from an Egyptian tombstone. AH 174 (790 AD). Museum of Islamic Art, Cairo. Simple Kufic is characterised by straight vertical strokes and angular forms of letters.

b). **Foliated Kufic** from a tombstone at Kairouan in Tunisia. AH 341 (952 AD). The vertical strokes end in leaves and half-palmettes.

c). **Floriated Kufic** from an Egyptian tombstone. AH 243 (848 AD). Museum of Islamic Art, Cairo. The ending of the letters is enhanced by the floral designs and half-palmettes, while the round forms are rendered as rosettes.

d). **Naskhi** from an Egyptian tombstone. AH 684 (1285 AD). Museum of Islamic Art, Cairo. Naskhi is a cursive form of Arabic writing, here the verticals are not so important; some of the foliation has been taken over from Kufic.

e). **Thuluth** from the drum of the Mausoleum of Princess Tughai in Cairo (died 1348 AD). Thuluth is a more cursive and more elegant form than Naskhi. The words are placed above each other in two or even more lines.

f). **Nastaliq** from the front page of Sadi's *Gulestan*, Bukhara. AH 950 (1543 AD). Gulestan Palace, Teheran.
In nastaliq the horizontal lines and round forms are exaggerated, dots casually placed, lines are not always straight, all of which make the nastaliq a very elegant form of writing.

pictures or the representation of living forms in Islam, and there is no mention of it in the Koran.

Certain pronouncements attributed to the Prophet and carried in the Hadith (the collection of traditional sayings of the Prophet) have perhaps been interpreted as prohibitions against artistic activity, although they are of purely religious significance. When saying that no angel will enter a house in which there are images, idols are meant, not figural representations. Artistic creation is perhaps included in a warning to the maker of images that he will be most severely punished on the day of judgment since he has tried to imitate God who alone can create living beings. He will be called upon to give life to his creatures, and, failing will be condemned. But even this statement seems to be directed mainly against idolatry rather than against artistic creation.

The fact remains that in practically no period of Islamic culture were figurative representation and painting suppressed, with the singular exception of the strictly religious sphere where idolatry was feared. Mosques and mausoleums are therefore without figurative representation. Elsewhere, imagery forms one of the most important elements and a multitude of other pictorial traditions were also assimilated during the long and complex history of Islamic art.

Umayyad Art

After Muhammad's death, the first caliphs were nominated and elected at Medina but soon a struggle ensued between two main factions—The Shiites (*Shiah* 'party of Ali', Muhammad's son-in-law) who regarded Ali and his descendants as the only rightful caliphs, and the Sunnites (*Sunna* 'path', the traditional practice of Muhammad as set down in the Hadith) who believed that the caliphate is an elective office open to any member of the prophet's tribe of the Kuraish (Qoraish). The family of Umayya of the Kuraish tribe emerged triumphant from this dispute and formed the first national dynasty of the Umayyads (661–750).

The Umayyads moved the capital from Medina to Damascus with the result that Muslim culture now had direct contact with late classical culture in the Roman provinces recently acquired by the Arabs. Umayyad art is characterised by the highly successful fusion of almost purely Roman and clearly hellenistic and Asian elements in which new interrelationships are created and entirely original forms of art evolved. In this fusion of cultural elements a process began that was to become typical of all Islamic art—that of merging, reformulating and producing something new out of widely varying artistic traditions.

ARCHITECTURE

The very first monument of Islamic architecture, the Dome of the Rock in Jerusalem, built by order of Abd al-Malik in 691, is a powerful example of this peculiar and quite original aspect of cultural galvanisation. Erected on a traditional pre-Islamic plan of a domed rotunda with ambulatories, it is at the same time highly original in its particular use of architectural and decorative elements. Basically 'Western' in tradition, it includes, particularly in its mosaic decoration and stone carvings, motifs of Eastern hellenistic (Sassanian-Persian) derivation, marking the beginning of a long line of hybrid art-forms.

The building is a political and religious monument, meant to establish right at the outset of Muslim rule, the final superiority of Islam over the 'people of the book', Jews and Christians alike, and in its location on the most sacred spot of the ancient world, symbolises the end of a tradition that was to be absorbed into the new culture of Islam.

The Dome of the Rock is in many ways a unique building, but in following an old prototype, it is the last manifestation of a pre-Islamic architectural form. In its decorative repertoire, however, it contains the germs for new and fertile developments in architectural decoration. Its great variety of motifs, ranging from the purely realistic, late classical, to the almost totally abstract 'modern Islamic', provides ample material for the pattern books used by craftsmen for the next fifty years to decorate the mosques and palaces of the Umayyads in Syria and Transjordan.

The Umayyad Mosque in Damascus, built between 705 and 715 into the remains of a Roman temple, introduces the most typical Islamic form of architecture—the open court mosque. This plan derives from the early encamp-

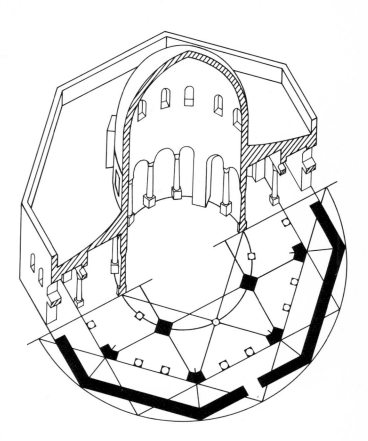

A. Plan of the Dome of the Rock, Jerusalem.

3. **Inner Ambulatory of the Dome of the Rock, Jerusalem.** Jordan. 691. This view shows the extraordinary richness of decorative detail, ranging from the marble incrustation and mosaic decoration of the pillars and arches to delicate gilded metal ornaments on the tie beams. The effect is entirely that of a late classical interior.

ment mosques of conquering Muslim armies, set up in the open field with nothing more to them than a ditch and a palm-trunk shelter on the kibla side. This simple concept of setting aside a primitively defined open space as 'place for prayer' seems to have determined once and for all the Arab form of mosque. Even though pre-Islamic basilical and palatial traditions enter into the design of later buildings, the original basic idea of a large open court, enclosed by simple arcades on three sides and the roofed-over prayer hall on the kibla side, remains unaltered throughout the Arab world and even forms the basic design of the Seljuk mosque in Iran.

In the Damascus mosque the old walls of the Roman temenos are used as the defining walls of the enclosure. Arcades in double storeys line the inner court on three sides, and a prayer hall, three aisles deep, appears on the kibla side, the aisles running parallel to the kibla wall. Even though there is a central aisle in the prayer hall cutting through the parallel aisles, at right angles to the kibla wall, there is no definite direction in the building design as a whole. The enclosure is considerably wider than deep, a characteristic that is retained in most Arab mosques throughout the history of Islamic architecture.

Deeply indebted to pre-Islamic tradition but of particular significance in the process of assimilation are the so-called 'desert castles' of the Umayyad period. There are many on record and excavations have made it possible to reconstruct their original form. With their often magnificent decoration in mosaics, wall-paintings and plaster carvings, they also provide the major source of information about Umayyad art.

These palaces did not serve as hunting lodges or desert retreats for the still desert-bound Umayyad rulers and nobles, as romantic interpretation has it, but as centres of economic development in now deserted but in Umayyad times fertile and highly prosperous estates. Their plan follows that of the Roman frontier fort of the region almost to the last detail. In fact, much of the technical detail in the sanitary installations, the thermae or bath-houses, and in the construction of walls, arches, apse-like niches and gate structures is almost purely Roman in design. But again, following the general trend within Umayyad culture, there is a strong Eastern element especially in the use of an entirely un-Roman, in fact, alien art-form—plaster decoration in coating, moulding and carving.

The plans of most of these palaces are designed around a central courtyard surrounded by arcades on two storeys. The outer almost square rectangular enclosure is fortified by massive corner towers and a series of semicircular towers along the sides. In the centre of one side is the heavily fortified entrance gate, often quite broad, and ascending to the full two-storey height of the building. Through this gate one entered a long hall that in turn opened into the inner arcaded courtyard. On the ground floor were usually the rooms for the entourage of the prince or ruler, and for the animals, while on the upper floor were the living quarters

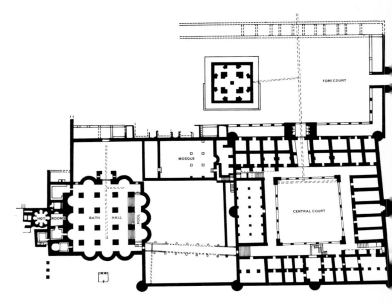

B. Plan of Khirbat al-Mafjar, Jordan Valley.

and the reception hall of the prince. This reception hall seems often to have been placed above the main entrance gate and to have been in many instances a domed chamber.

The two most important buildings that can be reconstructed from their remains, particularly in their decoration, are the palace of Khirbat al-Mafjar, in the Jordan Valley, east of the ancient city of Jericho, and the palace of al-Mushattah, in the desert south-east of Amman.

Khirbat al-Mafjar, probably built during the reign of al-Hisham (724–43), follows the usual plan of desert palaces just described, but is unusual in that it is not free-standing and forms part of a complex of buildings. There seems to have been a large open court surrounded by arcades on the east side, stretching the full width of the entire building complex which extends to the north, covering an even larger amount of ground than the main palace itself. These adjacent buildings enclose a mosque, a large court and an elaborately designed and very richly decorated bath-hall. A bath-hall adjoining a palace is not unusual but what is extraordinary is its specific elaboration into an independent almost monumental structure with a vaulted domed hallway and a large high gate decorated with figurative sculptures—among them one that may be a representation of the caliph himself. In the north-west corner of the bath-hall a small domed divan-hall is inserted which must have been the private audience and assembly room of the owner of the palace. The unusual importance of this part of the entire

4. **Façade of the castle al-Mushattah** in the Jordanian desert south of Amman. First half of the 8th century. Staatliche Museen zu Berlin. This richly decorated façade is unique in the art of early Islam and has often been ascribed to the pre-Islamic period. The rich variety of floral and animal forms in the carved stonework derive largely from classical sources. At the same time the stylised form of some of the animal motifs is unquestionably oriental, demonstrating the two sources of Umayyad art.

in having a huge basilical reception hall at the end of the main central court. This feature has recently been shown to have appeared in early Islamic architecture (Dar al-Imara, al-Kufah, Iraq) and seems ultimately to go back to Sassanian palace architecture rather than to local Christian basilical tradition.

Built on a different plan and probably following a different pre-Islamic tradition is the much smaller palace of Kusayr Amrah (Qusayr 'Amrah) not far from al-Mushattah. It has a single storey only, the principal buildings comprising a reception hall and an adjacent bath-house complex which again includes a dome chamber, painted with a zodiacal design—undoubtedly of symbolical rather than purely decorative significance. But the most important feature of Kusayr Amrah is its series of wall-paintings of which only fragments survive, but which have been well documented.

ARCHITECTURAL DECORATION

As already mentioned, the main elements of architectural decoration in Umayyad times are derived from late classical tradition: stone carving, mosaic floors, wall-painting, but added to these traditional forms is the new and—for Syria and Transjordan—alien form of plaster decoration.

The decorative stone carvings of most Umayyad buildings—capitals, door-lintels, cornices, etc.—follow almost without change pre-Islamic Roman tradition in form and execution. Mosaic floors uncovered in Khirbat al-Mafjar and al-Minyeh, also display a great variety of geometrical abstract patterns, mainly on a white ground, that have their immediate antecedents in late Roman and early Christian Byzantine buildings of the region. Most of the patterns can be found in Palestinian, Jordanese and Lebanese buildings of the 4th to 6th centuries, and there can be little doubt that ancient pattern books used by the artists of the region for generations continued in use throughout the Umayyad period.

Only one figurative floor mosaic has survived from the palaces—that in the small throne-niche of the bath-hall divan in the palace of Khirbat al-Mafjar. Its design—a group of grazing stags, and a lion killing a stag under a magnificent large fruit-bearing tree—has been interpreted as a symbol of royal peace and royal power under Islam. Its style is entirely in the late hellenistic tradition of naturalism, with the tree and animals in shaded colours to give an indication of roundness and depth.

This same tradition, stylistically and iconographically,

building complex is emphasised not only through its ambitious design but also by the fact that it seems to have been finished first, while large parts of the actual palace seem never to have been completed.

Both the floor of the divan-hall and an apse-like niche opposite its entrance are covered with mosaics, but while that of the rectangular chamber is abstract and linear, following the patterns of the magnificent floor mosaics of the main bath-hall, the mosaic of the niche is figurative and possibly symbolic in intention. It must have served as a kind of 'carpet' where the prince sat to receive his visitors. The rich stucco decoration includes four medallions with winged horses in the squinches and a row of small birds below the circular cornice of the drum. Both features may again have a symbolic value: they unquestionably add to the general impressiveness of a throne room.

The most important feature of the much larger palace of al-Mushattah is its unusual plan and its unique stone façade decorated with magnificent floral and figurative carvings. It is a monument of great beauty and accomplishment although, apart from the façade, no other decoration survives.

The majority of Umayyad palaces follow the plan of Khirbat al-Mafjar. Al-Mushattah is quite different. Beyond the entrance gate there is an inner court with adjacent buildings before the vast main court and the palace complex lies at the far end. It is particularly unusual

5. Mosaic decoration in the Umayyad Mosque, Damascus,
Syria, built 705–715 inside a Roman temple enclosure. This is
the earliest Arab mosque to have survived intact. With its rich
decoration in coloured marbles and polychrome mosaics, it
shows how late classical traditions continued without a break
into Umayyad times. The landscape mosaics have been
interpreted in various ways. The most likely explanation is that
they depict the world pacified by Islam.

was followed almost unchanged in the early mosaics of the
Umayyad mosque in Damascus, where idyllic landscapes
are depicted with a great variety of trees, and cities and
country palaces beside swelling rivers and splendid lakes.
Much of the iconography can be traced to late Roman
wall-paintings and mosaics, and some of the cities depicted
can be found in identical form in the 6th-century Justinian-
Byzantine mosaics of Ravenna.

It has been pointed out that these mosaics had a distinct
meaning for the beholder of the time, celebrating the
golden age of peace that began with the rule of Islam—
hence the open landscapes, open palaces, unfortified open
cities—and each architectural setting represented a specific place.

The earliest surviving Islamic mosaics—those of the
Dome of the Rock in Jerusalem—are curiously and characteristically enough the most hybrid. Combining classical
western and eastern hellenistic Sassanian elements they
demonstrate the complex nature of Umayyad art. There
are beautifully rendered fruit-bearing trees and magnificent
Roman acanthus scrolls, but there are equally prominent
palmette and candelabra trees of rather less classical, Sassanian inspiration.

Almost a complete pattern book of early Umayyad design is preserved in the beautifully executed open work
metal bands that decorate the undersides of the massive tie-
beams connecting the arches of the ambulatory-colonnade.
Here the gradual development from the purely late classical
motif of the grape-vine growing out of an amphora to the
semi-abstract, disconnected palmette patterns of eastern
hellenistic inspiration can be observed.

The most astonishing variety of patterns occur on the
numerous plaster panels that have been reconstructed from
fragments excavated in Khirbat al-Mafjar and Kasr al-
Hayr (Qasr al-Hayr). Again much classical inspiration is
evident, but Sassanian elements are now more dominant.
Here again the general development is clearly visible from
floral and growing plant decoration to the more separated,
stylised abstracted motifs, based on the naturalistic forms.
The surface is now divided more and more into geometrical
sections and filled with a repeat pattern of rosettes or single
palmettes, creating an effect altogether different from that
of the western, late classical world.

In the medium of plaster decoration Umayyad art
evolved a wide variety of sculptural forms, from compara-
tively low relief to sculpture in the round. Although always
forming part of a wall decoration (figures in niches, etc.),
some of these sculptures are astonishingly finely modelled,
embodying late classical developments in Central Asia,
Nabatean Transjordan and Coptic Egypt. Elements from
all three cultural environments seem to have been fused in
the stucco sculptures of the Umayyads.

(Continued on page 33)

1. **The Dome of the Rock, Jerusalem,** Jordan. Built by Abd al-Malik in 691. The Dome of the Rock is the first monumental building erected by the Muslims that has survived almost intact except for some later alterations, particularly in the exterior decoration (the tile revetments are part of the Ottoman restoration of the monument carried out in the middle of the 16th century). The building was erected as a religio-political monument and it is situated in the heart of the old temple district (the Haram al-Sharif) in the centre of the city. It is built above a rock, the Sakkra, the highest point of Mount Moriah, giving the building its name, Kubbat al-Sakkra. The complex symbolical significance of this rock and the particular location in the temple area were undoubtedly decisive in the choice of the construction site. The Dome of the Rock was for a time intended to become the substitute for the Kaaba—the sacred shrine of the great mosque at Mecca—as centre of pilgrimage for the Muslims. The plan, a round canopied shrine, follows pre-Muslim local tradition.

2. **The Great Mosque of al-Mutawakkil, Samarra.** 848–852. This is the largest mosque built by the Muslims. It shows the change from the classical architectural tradition of Umayyad architecture to the Eastern tradition of monumental brick construction. The huge minaret, with its external spiral staircase, inspired others (Abu Dulaf, Samarra; Ibn Tulun, Cairo) but did not create a type.

3. **Floor-painting from the Palace of Kasr al-Hayr, Syria.** First half 8th century. 10 ft. 8 in. × 8 ft. (3·25 × 2·45 m.). Damascus Museum. This painting from the Palace of Kasr al-Hayr in the Syrian desert was obviously a substitute for the mosaic decoration used in other Umayyad palaces (Khirbat al-Mafjar, al-Minyeh). In style and iconography it closely follows Roman models.

4. **Wall-painting from the Jausak Palace, Samarra.** 836–39. *Two Dancing Girls.* Reconstruction by Ernst Herzfeld. 19¾ in. sq. (50 cm.). This painting, only surviving in fragments (Museum for Turkish and Islamic Art, Istanbul), is one of many of court life from the ruins of the palace. The style seems to derive directly from Central Asian prototypes brought to Iraq by the Central Asian Turks.

5 (left). **Gold pitcher from Iran or Iraq.**
Second half 10th century. Chiselled
relief decoration on granulated ground.
h. (with handle) 6 in. (16 cm.). Freer
Gallery of Art, Washington. This is one of
the very few gold objects surviving from
the early Islamic period. Precious metal
objects have survived in small numbers,
not as often believed because they were
rare in Islamic art, but rather because
through their intrinsic value they were
vulnerable and therefore prone to be
destroyed. During the Buyid period a
special attempt seems to have been made
to re-create the style employed by ancient
Iranian silver and goldsmiths. Part of the
imagery of the relief decoration of this
small ewer—peacocks, ibex, and a winged
human-headed creature in medallions
formed of abstract floral motifs (palmette-
arabesques)—is directly derived from
ancient Persian tradition. The engraved
Kufic inscription along the rim mentions
the Buyid Amir Bahtiyar ibn Mu'izzad-
daula, who ruled in Iraq from 967 to 977.

6 (above). **Ceramic bowl from
Nishapur, Khurassan.** 10th century.
Slip-painted polychrome decoration.
diam. 14 in. (35·6 cm.). Museum of Art,
Cleveland. This is one of the best
examples of the peculiar figure style
developed in Nishapur pottery painting
of the 10th century. The origin of the
style, which has no parallel anywhere in
the Muslim world, is still unexplained.
Often purely decorative in intent, many
of these bowls are painted with what
would appear to be meaningful symbolic
subjects which in most cases have not so
far been satisfactorily interpreted. The
scene on this bowl has been identified as a
bacchanalia which harks back to classical
iconographical tradition; it has immediate
forerunners in Iran in the Sassanian
period.

7 (below). **Ceramic bowl from Iraq.**
9th century. Lead glaze and cobalt blue
decoration. diam. 8 in. (20·3 cm.).
Private Collection, New York. Muslim
potters were always fascinated by Chinese
pottery and porcelain. This bowl is
clearly inspired by white T'ang wares,
fragments of which have been found in
Samarra. But the Muslim ceramicists
were interested in colour and as their
technical limitations (running glazes, clay
bodies, low kiln temperatures) did not yet
allow underglaze painting, they used
glazes of different colours in an ingenious
way to achieve polychrome effects. The
use of blue on a white ground in this bowl
is the earliest occurrence of one of the
most popular forms of ceramic decoration
in centuries to come.

8. **Wall tiles from Ghazni,
Afghanistan.** 10th century. On loan
to the Metropolitan Museum of Art,
New York. Collection of Miss M. Schwarz,
N. Y. Recent excavations at Ghazni have
unearthed carved marble slabs and
tilework used in architectural decoration.
These tiles are typical of the general type:
monochrome glazed, they are decorated
with low reliefs of animal figures and have
a certain similarity to Chinese moulded
tiles of the Han period.

9. **Fragment of a wall-painting from
Nishapur, Persia.** Late 9th century.
h. 10¼ in. (26 cm.). Metropolitan
Museum of Art, New York. Few early
Islamic paintings in the East have
survived. These fragments demonstrate
the close connection between Persian
and Central Asian tradition at this time.
In the woman's face a great many Seljuk
features are anticipated: full roundness
of the face, almond-shaped slightly
slanting eyes, minute mouth and lobed
curls of hair across the forehead.

15. **Ceramic bowl from Iran.** 12th century. Underglaze painted decoration. diam. 7½ in. (19 cm.). Collection of Edmund de Unger, London. Black painting under a translucent blue or colourless glaze is a feature of pottery decoration that was first developed in Seljuk times. The use of both human and animal figures is common; the sphinx or harpy—the main element of the design of this bowl—is frequently encountered in Seljuk art in many media, but rarely has this fantastic creature been represented more skilfully. The quality of the design clearly indicates the close collaboration between master painters and master potters in the Seljuk workshops.

16. **Ceramic bowl from Kashan, Iran,** dated 1187 and signed by Abu Zayd al-Kashani. Polychrome overglaze painted decoration. diam. 8½ in. (21·6 cm.). Metropolitan Museum of Art, New York. Overglaze polychrome painted pottery of the so-called minai type belongs to the most beautiful and refined ware of the Seljuk period. Dated and signed pieces are rare, giving special significance to this bowl. The use of the nisba, al-Kashani, in the artist's name points to the place of manufacture of the piece, Kashan, and it numbers among a large group of minai ware that can be attributed to the workshops of that city. The subject is not altogether clear but it seems to represent a ceremonial procession scene of a prince with his entourage recalling a Mosul school painting (see plate 28).

17. **Ceramic bowl from Iran.** Early
13th century. So-called 'minai' ware.
Polychrome overglaze painted decoration.
diam. 18¼ in. (45·5 cm.). Freer Gallery of
Art, Washington. The painting on this
unique piece of minai ware undoubtedly
reflects a famous wall-painting in the
palace of the Seljuk rulers which has not
survived. The particular battle
represented and the individuals taking
part in it, even though many of them are
identified by name, is not known.

18. Ceramic plate from Kashan, Iran.
Dated jumada II AH 607. (November
1210 AD) and signed by Sayyid Shams
al-din al-Hasani. Lustre-painted
decoration. diam. 13⅞ in. (35·3 cm.).
Freer Gallery, Washington. The plate,
one of a small group of equally finely
painted pieces from the Kashan
workshops, is of particular interest as it is
not only dated and signed by the artist,
but also elaborately inscribed with Persian
poetry which throws some light on the
specific meaning of the scene represented.
The plate most probably belonged to a set
which included one piece showing the
ruler enthroned and surrounded by his
court. The scene on this plate probably
shows a royal groom, who has fallen asleep
and dreams of an adventure with a
mermaid-like creature who can be seen
in the water. He is supposed to be
guarding the ruler's horse; the people
behind the horse would belong to the
royal entourage. The piece is complex
both in subject-matter and in its
composition which is unusual in that it
extends beyond the confines of the piece
of pottery. It demonstrates the great
importance of the lustre-painted wares
from Kashan and is a key to our
understanding of painting in the Seljuk
period which has otherwise almost
completely disappeared.

19. **Painting from a copy of the
Warkah wa Gulshah poem.** Early
13th century. *Gulshah reveals herself to
Warkah who is led away as a prisoner.* 4¾ in.
(11·7 cm.). Topkapi Sarayi Library,
Istanbul. This is the only illustrated
manuscript that has survived from the
Seljuk period. Although it is not certain
exactly where it was made, it is a document
of major importance, proving the
existence of a school of book-painting in
the style known from minai painted
pottery of the 12th and 13th centuries
both in Iran and Anatolia. The painting

is a particularly fine example of the
highly decorative style developed by the
painter who has inscribed his name on
one of the paintings in this manuscript,
Abd al-Mu'min ibn Muhammad
al-Khoy al-Nakkash. His nisba would
indicate that he was from Azerbaijan.
Both the intricate design, placing the
figures against a background of a large-
scale palmette scroll, and the colour,
particularly the deep purples of the
background, are remarkable and
demonstrate the great sensitivity and
skill of this painter.

20. Ceramic ewer from Kashan, Iran.
1215. Black underglaze painted decoration. h. 7¾ in. (19·7 cm.). Metropolitan Museum of Art, New York. Seljuk potters excelled in extravagant techniques, constantly trying to give new

and special interest to their creatures. Some of their ceramic vessels are made with a double shell, the outer one being perforated to achieve a complete openwork pattern, a technique clearly derived from metalwork. Additional underglaze

painting and glazing in turquoise and cobalt blue make this ewer particularly appealing. The style of the figure drawing as well as the typical feature of a willowy scroll identify it as a product of the workshops of Kashan.

6. **Carved and moulded plaster decoration from Khirbat al-Mafjar.** Ceiling of the bath hall entrance-gate. Jordan. Mid 8th century. Jerusalem Museum. The extraordinary mixture of western and eastern traditions in early Islamic art is particularly clearly demonstrated in this work. While the acanthus rosette and the grape vine pattern of the frame are of purely western, Roman inspiration, the heads which form part of the design around the central rosette are of eastern hellenistic origin closely recalling Central Asian stucco sculpture of the 6th and 7th centuries.

PAINTING

No book painting from the first centuries of Muslim rule has survived, but enough wall-painting has come down to us, even though in a fragmentary state, to make an appraisal of this important and, apparently dominant art form possible.

The best preserved paintings of the period are the two floor paintings from Kasr al-Hayr. They demonstrate most clearly the typical duality of Umayyad art.

One of the paintings is entirely in the western classical tradition with a Roman motif—the earth goddess in a medallion with the symbol of a snake curling around her neck, and bearing fruit in a cloth. This central motif is surrounded by classical grape-vine scrolls and what have aptly been called maritime centaurs. The painting is in sombre greens, light browns, ochres and reds, with some touches of black and white, executed with a full brush. There is a considerable feeling for volume and space and the colours are applied in differing shades to give roundness and contrasts of light and shade to each form.

The second painting is of a completely different nature. Linear in design, divided into three horizontal sections, it is inspired by Sassanian painting in iconography and probably also in technique. In the upper part of the painting, under arcades of a non-classical nature, there are two musicians, while in the centre is a typically Sassanian hunting scene. Below, badly damaged, are the remains of what may have been a picture of the royal stables and deer-reserve.

Whether the contrast between western classical and eastern non-classical pictorial concepts in these two paintings was intentional and shows a contemporary awareness of the two major sources of inspiration is impossible to determine. The fact remains that these two paintings epitomise the cultural situation of the time. Other important fragments of wall-paintings from the palace have the same double style. Fragments of wall-paintings have also been found in Khirbat al-Mafjar, but the only other surviving series of paintings of any significance come from Kusayr Amrah.

Although largely destroyed, it is clear that the paintings of Kusayr Amrah formed a series of which the central theme was the glorification of the power of the Muslim ruler. Two of the surviving paintings in the reception hall illustrate this common theme particularly well.

One shows the enthroned ruler in frontal position, under a canopy resting on columns flanked by two attendants, one of whom seems to be holding a torch, while the other points towards the seated ruler. The ruler appears to be floating upon his throne between heaven—represented by the baldachin and a row of small birds all along the upper border of the painting which has an arcade shape—and the

7. Painting from the Palace of Kusayr Amrah, Jordan.
First quarter of the 8th century. The paintings of this small
palace show the continuation of late Roman iconography
and technique into the Islamic period.

8. Bronze ewer with engraved design from Syria. Mid-8th
century. h. 16⅛ in. (41 cm.). Museum of Islamic Art, Cairo.
This ewer was probably part of the treasure of the last
Umayyad Caliph, Marwan II. Its simple shape, fine linear
incised decoration and the high relief on the handle recall
Sassanian metalwork. The cock on the spout, however, follows
late hellenistic animal sculpture.

sea which is indicated below the throne. This is an un-
mistakable representation of the emperor as celestial ruler
of all the elements. (The bird motif is particularly noticeable, appearing in identical form in the dome of the divan-
hall, used as a royal reception room, in the bath-hall of
Khirbat al-Mafjar.) The other picture represents the conquered kings of the world that was subdued by Islam. Here
the Negus, the Byzantine Emperor, the Sassanian Shah,
and the king of the Visigoths, Roderic, are depicted frontally
performing gestures of submission and acclaim. The appearance of Roderic who was defeated and killed by the
Muslims in 711 gives a terminal date for the painting and
the building.

Mention has already been made of the zodiacal design
in the cupola of the adjacent bath-hall. A great many other
scenes also appear there, illustrating various aspects of
royal life and power, which seem to form part of a scheme
linking all the paintings and culminating in the scenes of
the glorified ruler in the reception hall.

The style is entirely classical. Rich colours put on with a
full brush show the immediate contact with late Roman
painting and a great many of the minor decorative details,
such as the grape-vine patterns, animal scenes, musicians
and herms that appear in the low vaults of various rooms in
the small palace, closely follow late classical prototypes.

DECORATIVE ARTS

Almost nothing of the decorative arts of the Umayyad
period has come down to us. Pottery seems not to have been
produced in any quantity as a luxury object; a little glass
has survived that would indicate a straight continuation of
late Roman glass production in Syria and Egypt, and possibly some of the earliest pieces of metalwork that can be
identified should be attributed to the Umayyad period.
Most of these pieces—ewers, and possibly some silver plates *8*
—are entirely in the Sassanian tradition.

Umayyad art, then, is the first manifestation of a new
cultural force in a world that is still fully under the spell of
late classical ideas. It makes use of traditional forms of
architectural design, but introduces new ones, as in the
mosque, that establish a tradition of their own. With the
use of plaster coating for architectural decoration, the re-
interpretation of various pre-Islamic traditions and the
creation of new formulae, the Umayyad period supplies
directives for centuries to come. The existence of a pictorial
tradition in Islamic art is already evident here, disproving
the common misconception that Islamic art is an iconoclastic culture. Both minor and monumental painting and
a highly developed figurative iconography appear already
in Umayyad art and lead to the first great school of known
Islamic painting, that of Abbasid Samarra.

The Abbasids of Baghdad and the Local Dynasties in the East

In 750 the Umayyad dynasty was replaced by the Abbasids who removed the capital from Damascus and Syria to Iraq, where Baghdad, the first major city entirely built by the Muslims, was founded by al-Mansur in 762.

Theoretically, the Abbasids held the reins of power until the middle of the 13th century when the last Abbasid caliph was killed by the invading Mongols in the sack of Baghdad in 1258, but in fact various parts of the empire were taken over by rival factions. Spain became independent under the Umayyads of Cordoba, and Egypt under the Tulunids (868–904). Both in the East and the West local dynasties established themselves and became independent from the central government in Baghdad.

The most important event of the early Abbasid period was undoubtedly the removal of the capital from Damascus —and a late classical milieu—to Iraq and the newly-founded city of Baghdad. With this the emphasis shifts decidedly towards the eastern tradition—the new capital even being built on an ancient oriental round plan—and a first step towards a final division between eastern and western Islamic art and culture was taken.

With the constant influx of Turkish peoples from Central Asia into western Asia and the gradual substitution of the Arab army by a Turkish military cast, a new chapter in the history of Islamic art begins. In the early 9th century this new phase was marked by the removal of the court from Baghdad to Samarra, a new city on the east bank of the Tigris a few miles further upstream. The art of Samarra was the first manifestation of an entirely new taste in Islamic art that ultimately derives from the Turks of Central Asia.

The importance of the Turkish element in Islamic art, not properly appreciated so far, cannot be overestimated. From the 9th century on, Turkish groups dominated vast regions of the Muslim world and imposed on them their peculiar, highly original, and altogether unmistakable taste. Even though in many instances Arabs, Persians, Greeks, Armenians, Syrians and Egyptians may have been

9. **Great Mosque, Kairouan, Tunisia.** 7th-century but rebuilt 836 and 875–902. One of the oldest monumental mosques of Islam and the first major monument in North Africa, this mosque follows Arab design in its basic plan while its decoration is largely late classical. Many of the columns and capitals were taken from pre-Islamic buildings. This view shows the prayer hall; the façade and the first dome over the central aisle are of the period of Ibrahim's enlargement of the building. The central aisle running toward the kibla wall and the mihrab is wider and higher than the other aisles, a principle already employed in Umayyad times, as in the mosque at Damascus.

10. **Minaret of the Great Mosque of Kairouan, Tunisia.**
9th century. The huge square tower, built in three sections with
a small crowning cupola, is one of the oldest minarets to have
come down to us. In plan and general design it may well derive
from Syrian church towers.

the craftsmen and artists that produced the actual artefacts
of Islamic art, it was the Turkish rulers and their vast
entourage that determined the form and content of that
art. The Turks brought with them artistic traditions that
merged with the local, eastern hellenistic traditions of Iraq
and Iran producing what is called the Abbasid style.

ARCHITECTURE

Nothing of Abbasid Baghdad survives. But its marvels
have been described so extensively that some sort of reconstruction is possible. The city, founded on August 1, 762, by
order of al-Mansur at an astronomically especially auspi-
cious moment, was built on a circular plan. There were four
gates at the cardinal points, and a vast central plaza. In the
centre of the plaza was the caliph's palace, the Kubba
(Qubba) al-Khadra, so called because of the tall green
dome that surmounted its centre. The dome could be seen
from a great distance and became the symbol of the capital
and of the rule of the Abbasids of Baghdad.

The fortification system was elaborate, with various deep
ditches round the city and five walls encircling the central
plaza. Between the third and fourth wall were the living
quarters so that the royal plaza was in the innermost part
of the city, separated by two walls with a wide ditch between them. A succession of heavily guarded gates, all with
complicated safety devices, protected the walls, with small
open courts corresponding to the width of the ditches between them. A long passage-way with forty bays of guard-
rooms linked the third to the fourth wall within the width of
the living quarters. The city thus had all the visible signs
of heavy fortification, an oppressive sight and certainly a
complete break with the open architecture of the Umayyad
period where, even in the 'desert palaces', the fortified
aspect was entirely decorative and non-functional. The
very idea of placing the royal palace in the centre of such a
succession of heavily guarded and fortified rings of protec-
tion is that of an oriental despot. Indeed much surviving
Abbasid architecture reflects this new concept of concentrated power in a vast and complex palace structure.

The form of al-Mansur's palace is not known, although it
is thought to have been similar to Sassanian palace designs
just as that of al-Mushattah and al-Kufah (see Umayyad
Art). Behind the palace was the great mosque—built, it
appears, entirely on the Arab court-mosque plan, the
prayer hall connecting directly with the palace in a way
that made the community of worshippers face the palace
when facing the kibla in prayer. In this feature the reli-
gious-political symbolism that governed some early Islamic
architectural design can be seen at work.

Of the vast city of Samarra which was founded by al-
Mutasim in 836, only two buildings survive, the mosque of
al-Mutawakkil, erected after 847, and the mosque of Abu
Dulaf, further east in the new quarter of the town and built
between 860 and 861. Nothing survives of the great palace
of the caliphs except the Bab al-Amma, the main gateway
that faces the river, but enough can be gleaned from the

11, 12. **Desert palace of Ukhaidir.** *c.* 120 miles south of Baghdad, Iraq. Late 8th century. This is the only palace to have survived almost intact from the early Abbasid period. Built with stone rubble set in heavy mortar and largely coated with plaster in the interior, the building has survived in a remarkable state of preservation. Its vast size alone makes it extremely impressive. The almost square enclosure measures some 575 × 555 feet (175 × 169 metres). It has heavily fortified outer enclosing walls, the palace being built against the north side. In design and construction it follows faithfully the local tradition based on ancient oriental models. It thus represents a complete break with the late-classical Umayyad architecture that preceded it.

remaining foundations to reconstruct most of the immense building complex. The plans of most of the larger houses can be reconstructed, and, although no plan of the entire city has been published, it would be no exaggeration to say that Samarra was probably the most magnificent city the Muslims ever built.

In contrast to Syria and Transjordan where stone was used exclusively, the building material of Iraq is unfired brick; only in special instances, for the coating of undecorated walls, arches or other structurally crucial elements, was fired brick used. This largely accounts for the disintegration of the city after it was abandoned at the end of the 9th century.

The great mosque of al-Mutawakkil was the largest ever built by the Muslims. Built on an immense rectangular plan (measuring about 784 × 512 feet) the massive, bastioned brick walls still stand more than 30 feet high. The minaret, perhaps the most famous 'object' of all Islamic architecture, and over 89 feet high, is set to the north of the enclosure. Built on a square base, the round tower tapers off towards the top. One ascends it by an external spiral staircase that gave the structure its name, al-malawiya (the winding tower). The plan of the mosque follows that of the Umayyad period, organised around a large open court.

13. **Mosque of Ahmad ibn Tulun, Cairo.** 876–879. The mosque adopts the principles of building construction brought to Egypt by Ibn Tulun from Iraq. Brick piers and plasterwork, both alien to Egyptian architectural tradition are used and in the ornamental plaster decoration of the arches, capitals, and the two mihrabs the dominant influence of Iraqi Abbasid art can be seen. The minaret of the mosque is an exact copy of the famous minaret of the Great Mosque in Samarra.

The most significant building of Samarra was undoubtedly the great palace, the Jausak al-Khakani, erected during al-Mutasim's reign, but added to in subsequent years. The huge complex covering 432 acres is probably the most ambitious building project ever undertaken by a Muslim ruler. Built in the tradition of the ancient Orient, the Jausak palace combines all the features of representational architecture that were developed in Iran and in Sassanian Mesopotamia (Iraq)—enormous ivan-halls, huge courtyards with water-pools and esplanades, domed throne rooms and complex intimate living quarters arranged around smaller courts with water basins and water courses, bath-halls and reception halls in ivan form on a smaller scale. The main element of the palace was the part that faced the river and of which the main triple gateway, the Bab al-Amma, is still standing. One approached it from the river level via a huge stairway. Its massiveness, complexity and size, and the extraordinary richness of its decoration **4** (some of the finest paintings and stucco decorations come from the Jausak palace), made this building one of the most extraordinary achievements of early Islamic art.

11,12 The only monumental structure that has survived from the first Abbasid period is the majestic palace of Ukhaidir, 120 miles south of Baghdad, in the desert on the Wadi Ubayd. It preserves in the most perfect form the ideal Abbasid palace. Unlike the Jausak palace, it is built of large unhewn stones set into mortar and, due to this method of construction, has survived almost intact. This palace is again modelled largely on pre-Islamic models of Sassanian inspiration. Immensely large and totally isolated in the middle of an uninhabited desert, the palace of Ukhaidir still communicates something of the grandeur of the people that built it. In its simplicity of form and restraint of decoration, limited to some highly original and fascinating plaster-coated vaulting systems with abstract geometrical patterns, it is one of the most beautiful of early eastern Islamic buildings to have survived.

ARCHITECTURAL PLASTERWORK DECORATION

For the decorative arts and paintings in the Abbasid period, we are almost exclusively restricted to the finds in the ruined city of Samarra. Of the elaborate plaster decorations of the palaces and mansions of the city, enough has survived to give us a complete idea of the extraordinary richness of imagination and originality of the art of Samarra.

Three distinct styles can be identified that later combine with a gradual change in technique. While the earliest phase of the Samarra style follows almost without change the late classical tradition, the middle phase draws away from the classical style. Finally in the third phase the truly original style of Samarra achieves its full expression.

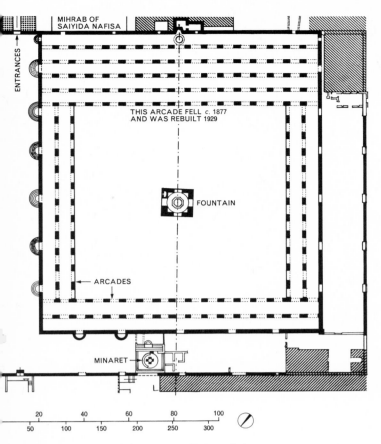

C. Plan of the Mosque of Ibn Tulun, Cairo.

The earliest plaster decorations are carved in high relief, deeply undercut, and depend for their effect almost entirely on the beautiful play of light and shadow, with sharp contrast between the brightly lit surface pattern and the impenetrably dark background. The patterns, consisting mainly of infinite variations of grape-vine scrolls, groups of decoratively arranged vine-leaves, acanthus scrolls and various other forms of floral ornaments, are cut by hand into the plaster in minute detail. Only thus could such a freshness and liveliness be achieved. Although often set within geometric panels or cartouches, the feeling for the natural growth of the plant form is always preserved. Only in rare instances does a purely abstract pattern penetrate into the still late classical concept of naturalistic ornament.

In the second phase the patterns become more abstract and the surfaces are filled tighter. Also a change from naturalistic floral growth to disconnected individually employed motifs, both floral and semi-abstract, often used in continuous repeat patterns, takes place.

In the third phase the final step towards complete abstraction is taken. While in the second phase some elements of the naturalistic late-classical ornament still survived, in the final stage all naturalistic form is eliminated in favour of a continuous abstract linear ornament that is entirely unclassical in feeling, and that changes the entire aspect of the decorative art of Samarra.

Also the technique changes. The patterns are no longer cut into the applied plaster but moulded which leads automatically to a continuous repetition of identical designs and does away with the light-and-dark contrast, the crispness and plasticity of the two earlier styles. The third style, without doubt, is due to a totally different attitude towards surface decoration and constitutes a complete break with the classical tradition.

The last Samarra style had an enormous influence on the way Islamic decorative motifs were treated in the ensuing centuries, not only in the East where it survived into the Seljuk period, but also in the West whither it was brought by the Tulunids, a Turkish slave dynasty in Egypt that became politically independent from Baghdad but depended artistically entirely on court tradition. In fact Ahmad ibn Tulun's mosque in Cairo, completed in 879, is modelled entirely on the great mosques of Samarra even to the point of having a spiral staircase minaret. The mosque is built in brick and decorated in the style of the last Samarra phase.

A number of tiles and tile fragments that have been found in the ruins of Samarra indicate that the plaster dadoes that decorated most lower wall surfaces, were at times combined with polychrome lustre-painted tiles. The important discovery of lustre-painting will be described later in the chapter.

The third form of architectural decoration widely employed was wall-painting, both of a decorative and a figurative nature—although mostly figurative.

WALL-PAINTING

The Samarra style of wall-painting, although undoubtedly rooted in Central Asia, combines Western and Eastern classical traditions in a particular way. The dominant element is a graphic style that ultimately seems to go back to Central Asia (Miran, 3rd century AD). A general immobility, even in scenes that represent action—a hunt, a struggle between man and animal, a dance—is a further altogether non-classical feature providing a strange contrast with the often classically inspired subject-matter. Perhaps the most interesting aspect of Samarra painting is the emergence of a facial type that had already made its appearance in Umayyad times, but became dominant only now. It seems to derive almost directly from an eastern hellenistic source which is best perhaps represented by the paintings from Miran.

The Samarra face is full and round with large, almond-shaped eyes with enormous pupils, a big, straight nose, only slightly curved at the very end, a small mouth composed of a very short straight line for the upper lip and a curved line drooping abruptly down at both ends for the lower lip. The hair is thick, black, and falls to the shoulders; it runs in a single scalloped line across the high forehead.

Most of the Samarra paintings have a linear quality. In a way they are more like coloured drawings than actual paintings, and are thus similar to the second floor-painting

14. Ceramic plate with relief decoration from Iraq. Early
9th century. diam. 11 in. (28 cm.). Freer Gallery of Art,
Washington. This is a typical example of the abstract linear style
of ceramic decoration developed in Samarra. The combination
of purely abstract interlace-band and floral elements is
particularly characteristic of the early Abbasid period. The use
of a very brilliant glaze with gold lustre elements is perhaps
intended to imitate metalwork.

**15. Ceramic bowl with lustre-painted decoration from
Iraq.** 10th century. Metropolitan Museum of Art, New York.
diam. 12 in. (30·5 cm.). Figurative subjects began to appear on
pottery only in the early 10th century. The lustre technique, a
new creation of the Iraqi potters, developed into one of the most
successful forms of ceramic decoration ever devised. It was
employed throughout almost the entire Islamic world until the
19th century.

of Kasr al-Hayr. Only on rare occasions is colour used without the deep contour-line that defines almost every shape.
The more pictorial style follows the technique of late
Roman painting and adopts late classical motifs. A striking
example of this type of painting is the large cornucopial
scroll from the Harim of the Jausak palace.

POTTERY AND LUSTRE-PAINTING

Pottery does not seem to have been produced as a luxury
object before the Abbasid period. The main stimulus was
probably the arrival of Chinese pottery in the Abbasid
court, for among the earliest vessels made in Baghdad are
those that imitate white T'ang ware, or the splash-coloured
pottery of the same period.

One ceramic group has fine relief-decoration of abstract
linear forms, at times ending in half-palmettes or using
decorative inscriptions, which find counterparts in China.
In Egypt the same wares bore figurative motifs—animals
and birds, in immediate reference to late classical iconography. But the most brilliant achievement of Baghdad
potters was the development of a technique that was to
revolutionise pottery decoration: the painting on the
surface of the glaze with a metallic pigment called lustre.

The lustre pigment, producing a metallic sheen on the
surface of the glazed and refired vessel, comes in shades of
green, yellow, brown and red and in the earliest and most
ambitious products of this new technique all those colours
are used on a single piece. The complexity of the process

and the great risk of failure, quickly resulted in the simplification of the polychrome lustre technique and a monochrome green-brown lustre took its place.

The lustre technique must have been a secret of the
potters of Baghdad because lustre-painting seems to have
been practised nowhere else in the Muslim world at this
early stage. In Nishapur, for instance, the cultural centre
of Samanid Khurassan, a great school of pottery had been
established in the 9th century, which together with Afrasiyab (Samarkand) in Central Asia became the leading
pottery centre in the 10th century. But in both cities lustre-
painting was unknown; they imitated openly the lustre
wares of Samarra but in a technique that could never come
near to the original lustre effect.

Polychrome lustre ware, it appears, was also made in
Tulunid Egypt but only abstract patterns, as in Samarra,
were used. Lustre pottery with figurative decoration appears only in the 10th century in Baghdad. The strange and
somewhat primitive style of the designs is due to a sudden,
strong influx of Central Asian traditions at that time.
There is an immediate similarity between some of the
figures on these lustre bowls and those on pottery made in
Nishapur.

BUYID ART AND ARCHITECTURE

At the same time as Abbasid culture reached its height in
10th-century Baghdad, a number of local dynasties established themselves in Iran, Khurassan and Central Asia,

creating important cultural centres of their own.

Among these the most important are the Buyids (or Buwayids), a Dailamite family that had maintained its independence from the central Muslim government in their region south of the Caspian Sea, and that had begun to take over large parts of western and southern Iran during the first half of the 10th century, reaching Baghdad before the middle of the century and forcing the caliph to resign from all political power.

Artistic life flourished under Buyid rule both in Iraq and Iran. Many important buildings were erected, among them the mosque in Nayin, which only partly preserves its original form—but which contains the only example of 16 plaster decoration on a large scale that has come down to us from that period. The plasterwork, still following in part late classical tradition in the grape-vine designs of the upper mihrab niche or the columns of the prayer hall, derives directly from the Samarra style.

The Buyids seem to have been particularly fond of fine and precious metalwork, an astonishing amount of which has been preserved. A complete silver treasure survives, probably made for a nobleman of Azerbaijan in the middle 17 of the 10th century. A quantity of silver plates with figurative scenes very much in the Sassanian tradition but clearly not in the Sassanian style, seem to have been made for 5 Buyid rulers both in Iraq and Iran. Two gold pitchers and some gold medallions bearing portraits of the rulers were almost certainly made for the rulers themselves.

Outstanding among the products of Buyid art are their magnificently patterned silks. Some are decorated with lengthy historical inscriptions while others combine the 18 calligraphic with the figurative element. Animal motifs dominate, but there are also representations of the human figure in stiff, formal hunting scenes. Most of the textiles are woven in two contrasting colours, brown, blue or black with a buff white. Most patterns are reversible—an astonishing technical feat considering the intricacy of the designs—so that there is either a light pattern against a dark ground or vice versa.

A variety of pottery types seem to have been made in the Buyid realm. Among them two with partly figurative representation stand out. The first employs a mainly linear incised technique with an almost monochrome colour effect not unlike some of the simple textile patterns. The glazes are dull brownish-white while the unglazed incised design appears dark, or light red. The second type is more complex. With its vividly coloured glazes and elaborate figurative designs, it follows even more closely the general trend of figurative iconography that seems to have been particularly strong in the Buyid period. Some of the usually solidly made large bowls are decorated with fantastic animals, human-faced quadrupeds or birds, others with scenes that seem to illustrate stories out of the *Shah-nameh*. If such interpretations are correct, we would have here the 19 earliest illustrations of Firdusi's poem, practically contemporary with the creation of the poem itself. This pot-

16. **Plaster decoration in the mosque at Nayin, Iran,** 10th century. In the prayer hall of this small mosque the earliest plaster decoration of Iran is preserved, following the tradition established about a century earlier in Iraq. During Buyid rule cultural relations between Iraq and Iran were very close.

17. **Silver plate with chased relief decoration from Iran.** *A Ruler enthroned with attendants and musicians.* 10th century. diam. 9⅞ in. (25 cm.). Hermitage, Leningrad. This plate is one of a large group of silver vessels that was long considered to be of Sassanian date but can now definitely be attributed to the period of Buyid rule in Iraq and northern Iran. Although they follow Sassanian precedents both in technique and iconography, they developed an unmistakable style of their own. Their low decorative relief, the often peculiarly Central Asian iconography and the static quality of their design are characteristic elements.

18. **Patterned Buyid Silk.** Persia. 10th century. Museum of Art, Cleveland. h. 19½ in. (49·5 cm.). w. 18⅝ in. (47·4 cm.). This is one of a large group of patterned silks that seem to have been made in or near Rayy for the Buyid rulers and princes of the 10th century. Their exceedingly fine technique, and often fantastic iconography place them among the most interesting and accomplished works of an art that seem consciously to have attempted to recreate the lost splendours of ancient Persian art. The motif of the design certainly goes back to at least the Sassanian period, and, although its meaning in Buyid times is difficult to interpret, it is not impossible that some of the symbolism, such as the particular representation of the bird of prey derives from an even earlier period.

19. **Ceramic bowl with carved relief decoration from Persia** (Garrus District). 10th century. diam. 6½ in. (16·6 cm.). Metropolitan Museum of Art, New York. The decoration of this small bowl is remarkable both for its technique and iconography. Low relief, achieved by carving the heavy slip coating, is common to a group of pottery found in the Garrus area. Human figures are not often depicted. The figure here is probably Dahhak, son of Mardas and king of the Arabs, who invaded Iran defeating and killing Jamshid Shah, making himself Shah of Iran. He is identified with evil forces and with idolatry. His curious attribute is a pair of snakes that grow from his shoulders. If this interpretation is correct, we have here one of the earliest representations of a scene from the *shah-nameh*.

tery, usually referred to as 'Gabri' ware, has survived in great quantity and must have been made somewhere in northern Iran.

SAMANID ART AND ARCHITECTURE

In Khurassan and Central Asia the Samanids had established themselves, creating in the cities of Nishapur in Khurassan and Afrasiyab (Samarkand) flourishing centres of the arts.

Little has survived of their architecture, but a mausoleum erected in Bukhara early in the 10th century provides *20* us with considerable information about their particular tastes and the special ability of the architects of the period. The small, square, domed building is entirely built of brick, a material that is used as a decorative medium. The entire surface of the tomb, inside and outside, is decorated with an abstract pattern created through a complex system of laying different layers of bricks in alternating positions. Dark recesses where light cannot penetrate emphasise an already powerful decorative scheme depending for its effect on contrasts between light and shadow. This is the first appearance of a formula that becomes central to the architectural decoration of the Muslim East.

The building is also the first example of a perfect 'canopy' mausoleum constructed in complete symmetry, each side being pierced by a pointed arch gate, recessed into the outer walls. The central dome is accompanied by four small decorative domes at the corners which do not appear in the interior. They correspond to four engaged columns at the four corners of the building. A curious gallery with a succession of small niches runs all around the top of the building hiding the drum of the main dome. This

20. **Mausoleum of the Samanids, Bukhara,** Transoxiana,
First half of the 10th century. This building, although of modest
size, is the most perfect example of a particular style of
decorated architecture. Constructed entirely of brick, the
surface patterns are achieved by alternating the direction and
position of the individual bricks or rows of bricks. The
mausoleum is the earliest major example of a style that seems to
have originated in Central Asia, penetrating thereafter the whole
of the eastern Islamic world.

21. **The Gunbad-i-Kabus, Iran.** 1006–7. This building, which is over 200 feet (61 metres) high, was intended not so much as a mausoleum, (although the King did intend to have his sarcophagus placed inside the tower), as for a symbol of political power. Highly abstract in form, and with a plain brick surface, the building contrasts strongly with the usually small, elaborately decorated tombs or victory towers then common to both Central Asia and Iran.

is again a feature that seems to be entirely original, and that was followed repeatedly in the centuries to come in various-ly elaborated forms in Central Asia, India and Iran. The building is one of the most remarkable monuments of early Islam, unique in the perfection of its design and in its importance for later developments.

Another unusual and highly successful architectural construction, the Gunbad-i Kabus, belongs to this period. It was erected by a minor local ruler in north-eastern Iran (Gurgan region) in 1007. Although planned to be used as a mausoleum, it was primarily erected as a monument of political power. Round in plan with a conical 'tent' roof, its only decoration consists of a series of inscribed panels be-tween the ten pointed-edge buttresses that run up from the base of the tower to the corbels that support the roof. The tower stands more than 165 feet high and measures almost 50 feet in diameter above the base. It is the largest building of its kind in Islamic architecture.

Although very little of the architecture of Nishapur has survived, a large quantity of decorative plasterwork from its buildings has been recovered in excavations. It is im-portant to remember that plaster decoration of architec-ture was used from the very beginning of Muslim rule right up to the Mongol period. At Nishapur the patterns, semi-abstract and floral, with leaf forms and arabesque palmette arrangements, follow very closely those of Nayin and Sa-marra, indicating a unity of style in a vast area that is quite remarkable. A general tendency towards flatness of surface, deep undercutting and elaborate decoration of the surfaces with small geometrical forms (triangles, polygons, etc.)—also seen at Nayin—prepare the ground for later develop-ments in the Seljuk and Mongol periods.

Very little of Samanid painting is known. The fragments of wall-painting excavated at Nishapur are largely orna-mental and also possess unusual quasi-magical qualities of an apotropaic (evil-averting) nature, it would appear. Stylistically they are not dissimilar from the abstract orna-mental paintings of 9th-century Samarra. The few frag-ments of figurative paintings that have been recovered reflect a tradition which can be traced back to Central Asian painting of the 6th and 7th centuries that was prob-ably of fundamental importance for early Islamic painting throughout the East and even influenced some western Islamic painting of the Seljuk and post-Seljuk periods.

The most important Samanid contribution to Islamic art is the school of pottery that flourished both in Nishapur and Samarkand. A great many types were produced, among them one with polychrome figurative representa-tion. The Samanid potters developed a polychrome under-glaze painting that would not run into the highly fluid glazes that were used at the time. To avoid the destruction of their designs by the running glaze they devised the ingenious plan of mixing their colours with parts of clay and earth to produce a substance similar to the slip (semi-fluid clay) that was put on the surface of an unfired clay vessel to smooth it and to give it a base for the application

22. **Plaster panel from Nishapur,** Khurassan, Iran. 10th century. h. 37½ × 8⅜ in. (186·5 cm. × 21·3 cm.). Metropolitan Museum of Art, New York. Plaster decoration, used since Umayyad times in architectural decoration, has not been recorded in Iran before the 10th century. The plaster panels recovered in the excavations in Nishapur are of the finest quality and, in their complex floral and abstract cut patterns, display close ties with the early Samarra style. They are remarkable both in the precision of the cut ornament and in the strict flatness of their surfaces.

of glaze. This 'slip-painting', as it has aptly been called, was an entirely new and original technique not known or used in other parts of the Muslim world.

The polychrome painted pottery of Nishapur preserves a style of painting that is not otherwise known but that very likely reflects wall and manuscript painting of the time. The usually small, heavily made steep-sided bowls are covered with a buff slip upon which dense, all-over patterns of animal groups, human figures, and abstract floral designs are painted in bright yellow, green, black and purple. Often the main motif—a seated figure, a horseman, an animal group—is surrounded by small-scale floral or animal motifs filling the entire background in an unsystematic way.

A second type of Nishapur pottery, also produced in Samarkand, is of different nature. Only two colours are used—white for the ground and black, dark brown or purple for the patterns. The designs are always abstract and in most cases calligraphic. Magnificent use is made of the beautiful Arabic script. Often single lines of a fine, very stylish calligraphy runs across the surface of the bowl, or a single word appears in the centre. The most accomplished

23. Ceramic bowl with decoration from Nishapur,
Khurassan, Iran, 10th century. diam. 18$\frac{1}{16}$ in. (45·8 cm.).
Freer Gallery of Art, Washington. This bowl is probably the
finest of a group of highly sophisticated ceramic vessels that are
decorated with elements of calligraphy in black and purple on a
white or yellowish ground. Complete inscriptions, written in a
peculiar form of kufic script that has an astonishingly close
relationship to the forms of the Uighur writing of Central Asia,
often appear on such vessels. This is the first time that the Arabic
script is used as a major element in surface decoration.

24. Ceramic bowl with slip-painted decoration
Nishapur, Khurassan, Iran. 10th century.
diam. 13$\frac{1}{2}$ in. (34·3 cm.). Metropolitan Museum of Art, New
York. Lustre-painting was obviously unknown in Nishapur
and the Samanid potters developed a slip-painted decorative
style that imitated the brown monochrome character and certain
other features, such as the 'peacock-eye' motif of the Iraqi
models.

examples have large-scale letters in a special form of Kufic
writing that has an extraordinary similarity to the form of
Turkic Uighur calligraphy; often one or two lines of writing run round the rim of these large, finely potted deep
bowls or flat plates. The glazes are brilliant and quite pure
even though they have a tendency to crack and loosen from
the ceramic body. A great variety of types exists within this
group and additional colours, especially a bright red, are
sometimes used for the inscriptions or palmette designs that
appear either in combination with the inscriptions or by
themselves. It seems that these 'polychrome' pieces were
mainly made in Samarkand.

It is astonishing to find that the obviously highly accomplished Samanid potters did not master the lustre
technique. The result was the production of a type of
24   pottery that imitated lustre in a greenish- and reddish-
brown slip painting without, however, being able to match
the special effect of the original technique. Some of the
Samanid potters' imitation lustre pieces also have patterns
which are clearly copies of Iraqi lustre ware.

The art of the Early Abbasid period reflects the political
situation of the time. With the removal of the capital from
the sphere of influence of late classical tradition, eastern,

and eventually Central Asian traditions began to play a
dominant role. The line of royal palatial architecture of
Sassanian Iraq and Iran was continued. Eastern hellenistic
and Asian elements mingled to create both a style and an
iconography in painting that were basically non-classical
and became of crucial importance for the further development of Islamic art. The general tendency towards an
abstract use of classical naturalistic ornament formed the
basis of all Islamic floral design, was brought to its first high
point in the 'bevelled style' of Samarra, transmitted to Iran
by the Buyids and adopted in Samanid Khurassan and
Central Asia.

The unity of the Umayyad style was replaced by the
complex style of the eastern Islamic development, reflecting the complex ethnic and political situation of the eastern
empire in the 9th and 10th centuries. Abbasid art forms,
particularly in the realm of pictorial representation and
abstract ornament, invaded western Islam through the
Tulunid expansion of the Abbasid realm to the West.

With the development of lustre-painting, the early Abbasid period made a fundamental contribution to the art
of Islam as a whole, providing further generations, as we
shall see, with a most effective means of realising the main
objective of most Islamic art, the dematerialisation of
matter and the sublimation of this world.

The Umayyads of Spain

While in Persia and Central Asia the local cultural centres produced art forms of great imagination and variety, the only survivor of the Umayyad family, Abd al-Rahman I (756–88), established an independent kingdom in Spain. Spain had been conquered by the Arabs early in the 8th century but it was not before Abd al-Rahman's coming to Cordoba that the country achieved significance within the general development of Muslim art and culture. During the three hundred year rule of the Umayyads, Spain and Cordoba became the most important cultural centre of the Muslim world, rivalled only by Baghdad. The open rivalry between Cordoba and Baghdad manifested itself in the proclamation of the western caliphate under Abd al-Rahman III (912–61) in 929.

Although Cordoba always remained the centre of the Umayyad realm and its great mosque, founded by Abd al-Rahman I in 785, was constantly enlarged and enriched during the reigns of his successors, a palatial city, Madinat al-Zahrah, was built by Abd al-Rahman III and enlarged by al-Hakam II in the 10th century. It was during the reign of these two men that Cordoba became the equal of Baghdad and Umayyad power reached its greatest height in Spain and North Africa.

ARCHITECTURE AND ARCHITECTURAL DECORATION

D The great mosque in Cordoba is to this day one of the most remarkable monuments of Islamic architecture. Designed on the traditional Arab mosque plan, it consisted originally of a large rectangular enclosure of which the larger part was an open court with a covered prayer hall on the south side. This relatively simple building was enlarged four times in the following centuries; Abd al-Rahman III had a tall minaret added to the mosque around 950. But the most important modification of the building was that of al-Hakam who had seven aisles added south of the prayer hall. During the period of al-Mansur both the court and prayer hall were extended westwards. The present building is the third largest mosque in existence after the two at Samarra.

The court to the north is surrounded by open arcaded porticos; to the south the vast prayer hall has nineteen aisles, its roof resting on eighteen double-storey arcades running perpendicular to the kibla wall. Al-Hakam's new kibla wall is the most splendid part of the mosque with its

11 mihrab magnificently set off by a number of highly sophisticated 'cappellas'. With this addition Hispano-Islamic art reached its highest achievement only to be matched by the Alhambra in Granada three hundred years later (see Nasrid Art). The lavish architectural design, the creation of the double- and triple-arch arcade, the extraordinary versatility in decorating the surfaces of the arches and niches, the mihrab and the cupola of the *Cappella del mihrab* with stucco and mosaics, the variety of designs employed and the perfect equilibrium between the richness of detail and the tranquillity of the total effect, is perhaps unparalleled in early Islamic art.

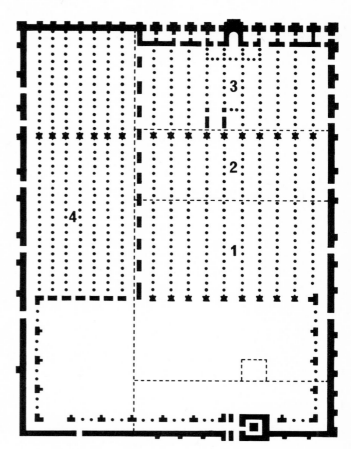

D. Plan of the Great Mosque at Cordoba in the tenth century. 1. Mosque of Abd al-Rahman I; 2. Addition of Abd al-Rahman II; 3. Addition of al-Hakam II; 4. Addition of al-Mansur.

The plaster and marble decorations in the mosque—which can be compared with those of the city of Madinat al-Zahrah—are as delicate as lace. The flat patterns, all based on classical naturalistic motifs, are reduced to a brilliant, precise tracery against a dark background.

DECORATIVE ARTS

The same technique of precisely cut floral ornaments on a fairly flat surface against a deeply receding dark background is used in the many fine ivory carvings of the period. As many of these pieces are dated, or datable through historical inscriptions, a perfect chronology can be established for the development of the style. While the earliest pieces are almost exclusively floral-abstract, later objects include quite complex figurative designs with interesting subject-matter. A group of silk brocades, probably made in Almeria, proclaim the open rivalry with Baghdad. Although none of the ivories are thought to have been made in Baghdad, (as were two of the Spanish silks), some of the royal iconography employed has a clearly eastern Islamic connotation imitating typically Abbasid concepts of representational art, strange in a country that regarded no one with more enmity than the Abbasids of Baghdad.

25a,b,c

25a, b, c. **Ivory box with carved relief decoration.** Made for Abd al-Malik in 1005. *c.* 10 × 20 in. (25·5 × 50·7 cm.). Cathedral Treasury, Pamplona. Ivory carving had been highly developed in Umayyad Spain and figurative representations, often following Iraqi models, were widely used. Abd al-Malik's carved ivory box is an outstanding example of this art.

The art of Umayyad Spain is the first manifestation of the new 'Islamic' attitude towards classical tradition in the West. Almost entirely unaffected by the impact of Central Asian tradition that was changing eastern Islamic art at the time, Spanish-Islamic art found a highly original way of adapting the traditional forms of classical architectural design (the double arcade of the mosque in Cordoba, for instance, was probably developed directly from the Roman double-storey aqueducts in Spain) and classical naturalistic ornament, to a new, and in its ultimate realisation, entirely non-classical taste. Spanish-Islamic art achieved in its first period a character of its own that it was never to lose. This consists of a strong tendency towards abstraction on the basis of an always clearly definable individual form. Naturalistic motifs are never abstracted to the point of becoming unrecognisable. In this Hispano-Islamic art does not follow the principles established in 9th-century Iraq, even though most of its figurative repertory is derived from there. The most remarkable achievement of this art was an extreme refinement both of design and technique which was applied to all forms of decoration. A unity of style was created, embracing both the monumental in architectural stone, marble and plaster carving, and the minute, in the carving of small ivory boxes and panels, a feature that is typical of Islamic art in general, but was developed to a particularly high degree in Umayyad Spain.

(Continued on page 65)

21. **Karatay Madrasah** (entrance).
Built by order of the Amir Celaleddin
Karatay, grand vizir of Kay Kaus II in
1251. Konya, Turkey. Only the entrance
portal and the main dome chamber of the
madrasah survive. The portal is a fine
example of Seljuk decorative stone
carving and the use of different coloured
marbles for decorative purposes in
architectural surfaces. The Karatay
Madrasah is one of the finest
surviving examples of the dome chamber
type of building. The interior is
particularly richly decorated.

22. Carpet from the Mosque of Alaeddin Kaykubad, Konya, Turkey (detail). 13th century. (Whole rug) 17 ft. × 9 ft. 4 in. (5·2 × 2·85 m.). Museum of Turkey and Islamic Art, Istanbul. The superb balance of colour and design is typical of early Turkish carpets. This detail shows the strikingly bold border design, based on elements of kufic writing and a corner of the field filled with an infinite pattern of interconnecting abstract floral scrolls.

23. Interior of the Mosque of Alaeddin Kaykubad. 1220 AD. This is the major mosque of the Seljuk rulers in Konya, their capital in Anatolia (Turkey). This view shows the colonnades of the prayer hall running parallel to the kibla wall and the use of rugs. These are modern replacements of the oldest surviving ancient rugs (see plate 22).

24. Enamelled brass basin (inside). Made for an Urthukid Seljuk ruler, d. 1144, diam. 9 in. (23 cm.). Ferdinandeum, Innsbruck. Very few pieces of metalwork made for the Urthukids survive and this is the only known piece of Islamic metalwork with enamel decoration. Immediate contact with Byzantium accounts for its technique and the way Alexander is elevated on his 'throne' (the chariot) by 'eagles' (the winged griffins), a motif directly deriving from Byzantine models.

25, 26. **Aleppo citadel, Syria.** *c.* 1210, with later additions. Built at the top of a hill that dominates the city of Aleppo, the citadel is one of the most remarkable buildings of civic Islamic architecture. The photographs show the formidable entrance gate-tower and the bridge that crosses a deep ditch to the actual gate, a massive tower on the slope of the hill. This building, a masterpiece of Syro-Islamic architecture in its classical simplicity of form and complexity of design, was erected by the Ayyubid Sultan Malik Zahir Gazi (there are two inscriptions in his name, dated 1209 and 1212 respectively).

29 (left). **Ceramic vase from Damascus, Syria.** Late 13th century. Lustre-painted decoration. h. *c.* 12 in. (30·5 cm.). Collection of the Marquis de Ganay, Paris. Following the form and basic design established in Syria in the first half of the 13th century, this vase combines in an original way the use of a dark coloured background (glaze) with yellow lustre decoration. The combination of small-scale leaf-scroll background decoration and large-scale interlaced pattern is equally original.

30 (above). **Ceramic vase and ewer from Rakka, Syria.** 13th century. Ewer: h. 9¼ in. (23·5 cm.). Vase: h. 7⅛ in. (18·1 cm.). Metropolitan Museum of Art, New York. These ceramic pieces represent the two most popular forms of pottery making and decoration developed in 13th-century Syria: black painting under a greenish-blue glaze and lustre-painting. The pear-shaped vase is typical of Syrian pottery and goes back several centuries; the small lustre jug is an equally original creation of Syrian potters but apparently does not appear before the 12th century.

The close contact between Syrian and Persian pottery can be seen particularly in the design of the half-palmette-leaf scroll and the whirl motif of the lustre-painted jug. With the destruction of Rayy by the Mongols in 1220, many Seljuk potters fled Iran and found new employment in Syria giving new impetus to ceramic making there.

31. **Painting from a copy of Hariri's Makamat.** Syria. 1222. Bibliothèque Nationale, Paris. The painting demonstrates the close relationship between the Syrian school of painting in the early 13th century with Byzantine and western, non-Islamic tradition. Contemporary and earlier Christian paintings must have served as models for the painters of this manuscript in particular as they seem almost entirely free of eastern Islamic influences. Miniatures of this type have justly been called hellenistic rather than Islamic in feeling.

وَكَادَ يَنزَعُ الجِمَالَ النَّمَرَ والنَّشَدَ

مَا الحِجُّ يَبرَكُ تَأويبَاً وإدلاجَاً وَلا اغتِيامَكَ أجمَالاً وأحدَاجَا

الحجُّ أن تقصِدَ البيتَ الحرامَ على تَحريمِ بَيدِكَ الحجُّ لا تَبغي بِهِ حَاجَا

وَتُعطِيَ كُلَّ أهلِ الإنصافِ مُتَّخِذاً رَدعَ الهَوى بِاديَاً هَاديَاً والحَوزُ مِنها شَاجَا

32. **Painting from a copy of Hariri's Makamat,** Baghdad, Iraq. 1237. *Pilgrim Caravan.* 10 × 10½ in. (25·3 × 26·7 cm.). Bibliothèque Nationale, Paris. The illustrations of this codex form the main work of the Baghdad school of painting. They demonstrate the extraordinary impact of hellenistic painting. Although there was undoubtedly a continuous tradition of painting in Baghdad following late classical models, only 13th-century examples survive. The realistic representation of animals and human figures and choice of subject-matter from the actual life of people of the period is rare in other Islamic painting.

33. **Kuwwat al-Islam Mosque, Delhi, India,** built by Kutb al-din Aibak in his fortress of Lalkot near Old Delhi, 1193–1210. This mosque is the earliest surviving monument of Islamic architecture in India. In its combination of local, pre-Muslim traditions and imported architectural forms, it is typical of the earliest period of Islamic architecture in India. The mosque is built on to the ruins of a Jain temple, in front of which a screen wall with a large central pointed archway and smaller, lateral arches was built. The decoration is mainly carved low relief.

34. **Pir-i Bakran, Linjan,** 30 km. S.W. of Isfahan. 1299–1312. Mausoleum of Shaykh Muhammad ibn Bakran, d. 1303. This small building was originally intended as a religious school consisting of a monumental ivan hall but was then changed into a mausoleum through the curious device of closing the open side of the ivan hall with a screen wall. It is particularly remarkable for its outstanding plaster decoration in which all the possibilities of Mongol architectural decoration are explored and applied. The astonishing variety of form ranges from plain, flat coating with linear incised designs, forming continuous patterns both abstract and epigraphic, to the almost baroque movement of the highly complex multiple level of the mihrab. The illustration shows one of the deep niches in the sides of the ivan hall walls, decorated with an abstract arabesque ornament recalling designs first developed in 9th-century Samarra.

35 (right). **Painting from Manafi al-Hayawan** (*The Usefulness of Animals*) a copy by Abu Sa'id Ubayd Allah ibn Bakhtishu. Maragha, Iran, between 1294–99. *Adam and Eve.* $13\frac{1}{2} \times 9\frac{3}{4}$ in. $33 \cdot 5 \times 24 \cdot 5$ cm.). Pierpont Morgan Library, New York. The paintings in this manuscript are the earliest known from Mongol Iran. Some clearly show the dependence of the Mongol painters on earlier models. This painting is of particular interest not only because representation of semi-nude human figures is rare but also because of the obvious fusion of at least two pre-Mongol painting styles: that of the Baghdad school which contributed the landscape element, and that of the Seljuk schools, which provided the models for the figures.

قال التّماری الجذر منافع من وزن

اول بذانكه جون نطفه
دزرحم ماده حاصل شود
وقوا زكبرد ومنیأز
قوّت وحرارت
بیذا كردد واز دماغ
ودل وجكر بیاید
ونفس كلّی بذان رسد
ما اند زرده خایه باشد
دم الطمث باز بندد
وهم جون سپیده خایه
نرا منسر دزاید جنانك

بنیزمایه اندرسپیذ تازه بیر علقه كردد ما ما اول دزتدبیز نطل باشد واز بهرانك طبع دجلوونطفه

وبرونددرنراییه که اندرنراییه ازبعدسه دورُ بدیدآید وبه ازاسبیده خیزد وزددخوردو طعمه اوباشد

اندرصورت سیمرغ

سیمرغ اندردماراو محیط باشد اندرجزیرها بنردکی خط اُستوا ومردم بدان جای نشیند وهوای خوش دارد

36 (left). **Painting from Manafi al-Hayawan** (*The Usefulness of Animals*) by Abu Sa'id Ubayd Allah ibn Bakhtishu. Maragha, Iran, between 1294–99. *The Phoenix.* 13½ × 9¾ in. (33.5 × 24.5 cm.). Pierpont Morgan Library, New York. This painting from the earliest surviving Mongol manuscript shows the important influence of Far Eastern art on the development of the Mongol style. Not only the subject, the phoenix, but also the use of a great many conventions, such as those for the representation of trees, flowers, water and clouds, are largely inspired by Chinese paintings.

37 (above). **Painting from a copy of Firdusi's Shah-nameh** (Book of Kings). Tabriz (?), Iran. *c.* 1380. *Bahram Gur having killed the wolf.* page: 16¼ × 11¾ in. 14.3 × 29.8 cm.). Fogg Art Museum, Cambridge, Mass. The illustrations of this dispersed copy of a *Shah-nameh* differ greatly in style and quality. Some have close ties with the early Mongol school, others anticipate the Timurid style. This is one of the most successful paintings of the series, combining almost magically realistic detail with an element of ceremonial symbolism, a combination typical of a large number of paintings in this manuscript.

38 (left). **Painting from a copy of Firdusi's Shah-nameh** (Book of Kings), Shiraz, Iran. 1341. Made for the Vizir Hasan al-Kivam al-daula wa'l-din, vizir of the Inju rulers of Shiraz. *Shapur surprising a Chinese Woman at a Well.* 13 × 10¾ in. (33 × 27·3 cm.). Fogg Art Museum, Cambridge, Mass. This painting illustrates the typical features of the style of the Shiraz school in the Mongol period which differs fundamentally from that of the metropolitan style developed in Tabriz. There is a special emphasis on linear effect and the colours are thin, soft, and kept to a limited palette of reds, browns, yellows and soft blues. The paintings have often the quality of tinted drawings rather than actual paintings and they are sometimes rather sketchily, even carelessly executed.

39 (below). **Painting from a copy of Amir Khusrau Dihlavi's Khamsa.** India. Middle of the 15th century. *Majnun throws himself on Layla's tomb.* 5 × 8½ in. (12·7 × 21·6 cm.). Freer Gallery of Art, Washington. This painting comes from a now dispersed manuscript which can be attributed to the Sultanate period in India on the basis of iconographic details which are typically Indian and do not appear elsewhere in Islamic painting. The intensity of colour and the bold, simple design are without immediate parallel outside India, while there seems to be an obvious link with contemporary Rajput painting. Contacts with both the Inju and Mamluk schools of painting may also have been equally instrumental in the creation of this particular style.

40. **Ceramic plate from Iran.** 14th century. So-called Sultanabad district ware. Underglaze painted decoration. diam. 12¾ in. (33·6 cm.). Lehmann Collection, New York. The representation of human figures is rare on Mongol pottery. The decoration of this plate is typical of the so-called Sultanabad ware, possibly of Kashan, in the use of two colours, green and blue. The group of figures is obviously taken from an illustrated manuscript of the period, or rather, executed by the same masters that illustrated the copies of Rashid al-din's *History of the World* and similar works of the early Tabriz period of Mongol rule.

The Fatimids

After the fall of the Tulunids (905), a period of political chaos caused a rapid decline in the cultural life of Egypt. Only with the Ikhshidids (935–69) was order once more established so that a new development of the arts and crafts could begin. Then, during the period of Fatimid rule (969–1171), Egypt took the lead in the cultural life of western Islam.

The Fatimids, a Berber dynasty that had incorporated Egypt into their North African empire (formed at the beginning of the century, and subsequently lost when they removed the capital from al-Mahdiya, near Tunis, to Cairo), established an independent caliphate, being of the Shiah faction of Islam as opposed to the Sunnites of Baghdad. The Fatimids brought to perfection an artistic tradition that they had inherited from Iraq—figurative representation. In painting, wood and ivory carving, and even on glass, crystal, and textiles, a multitude of figurative subjects appeared that is unparalleled in Islamic art at that time.

ARCHITECTURE

Although nothing has survived of the two great Fatimid palaces in the centre of Cairo which faced each other across a large square, descriptions of them give some idea of their wealth and magnificence. The façade of the larger Eastern Palace—finished in 973—had nine monumental gateways. The Lesser, or Western Palace was completed only at the end of the century.

The earliest Fatimid mosque in Cairo, al-Azhar (970–2), although considerably altered in subsequent centuries, still retains enough of its original form to convey the special quality of early Fatimid religious architecture. The plan follows that of the standard Arab mosque, adopting the central, slightly elevated aisle in the prayer hall, emphasised through double columns that carry the pointed arches supporting the roof, and including two domes in front of the mihrab, a feature known from the mosque of Sidi Okba in Kairouan (Qairawan).

The great mosque of al-Hakim (996–1020), begun by his father but completed only in 1013, is an immense rectangle, with two tall minarets at the western and northern corners and the monumental main gateway between them. Other gateways appear in the centre of each side. The court is surrounded on three sides by open arcades. On the fourth is the large five-aisled prayer hall with an elevated central transept to the kibla and a dome in front of the mihrab. Similar domes appear in the southern and eastern corners of the prayer hall. The building closely follows the design of Ibn Tulun's mosque; the piers that support the roofs are even constructed in a manner similar to that of the earlier mosque with rough masonry, and one of the tie-beams in the transept is still decorated with an abstract floral pattern that follows directly the Tulunid tradition as derived from Samarra. Only very gradually did a new floral and particularly an abstract linear style of decoration develop. The new decoration can be seen on some carved stone orna-

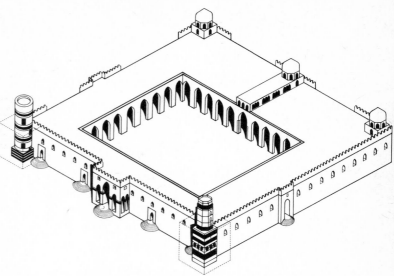

E. **The Mosque of al-Hakim in Cairo.** 990–1013. Reconstruction of the original state (after Creswell). The Mosque of al-Hakim, following a tradition established in Egypt with the Mosque of Ibn Tulun, which in turn was directly derived from Abbasid Iraq (Samarra), is the outstanding example of religious architecture of the Fatimid period. Constructed mainly of stone, but also using brick as a building material, it combines and fuses the various building traditions in Egypt into a new unity. With its large scale, pronounced accent on the façade through a massive central gate-way and corner-tower minarets, the mosque achieved a monumental effect that was typical of Fatimid architecture.

26. **Conch-shell motif on the façade of the Mosque of al-Akmar, Cairo.** 1125. Fatimid architecture excelled in massive stone construction and large, blank surfaces placed in contrast to the deep-cut, powerfully carved design of an almost exclusively abstract nature. In its perfect balance of individual features and precise carving of both the conch shell motifs and the inscription bands, the façade of al-Akmar is a masterpiece of its kind.

ments in the passageway leading through the main gate to the inner arcade and court.

Calligraphic elements became of great importance in architectural decoration; inscriptions appear around the windows and niches in narrow framing bands. The minaret towers in particular—one cylindrical, the other octagonal on a square base—are decorated with bands of kufic writing, abstract interlaced patterns and open grill windows.

One of the finest examples of this new and vigorous style of stone carving in architectural decoration is the façade of the mosque of al-Akmar which was completed in 1125. The façade, part of which is hidden today by modern houses, is characterised by a highly abstracted angular version of the conch shell motif known from late antiquity and used in a large number of early mihrab niches. The particular form used here had been developed in Egypt, it seems, and can be specifically associated with the Fatimid period. Along the top of the façade is a beautifully carved inscription. A second narrow inscription band runs below. Minor decorative elements, such as small disks or squares filled with abstract ornaments, complete the simple but impressive design.

POTTERY AND PAINTING

Fatimid painting is mainly known through figurative decoration on pottery. Outside of Egypt a single major monument produced by Fatimid artists, has survived, the ceiling of the Cappella Palatina in Palermo.

Little is known about Egyptian pottery before the Fatimid period. The Tulunids had apparently imported potters from Iraq and with them a tradition of fine ceramic making was introduced. Fatimid vessels, mainly fairly large bowls and plates, are solidly made, nor are the shapes very elegant. The glazes, of a creamy white, are thick and tend to crack and dull easily. The main interest of this pottery lies in its decoration, painted in deep brown lustre. A variety of floral and figurative patterns of great beauty demonstrate clearly the transmission of the Samarra style to the West.

A number of different styles can be distinguished and even artists' names are known. Although dated pieces are virtually non-existent, a certain chronology can be established. The earlier style follows exclusively the Samarra tradition in its heavy outline drawing, simplicity of iconography and conscious contrast between the main object of representation (usually a single figure) and the decorative background. The main motif is set off by irregularly shaped panels that follow the outline of the given figure represented, using up the undecorated space of the background, not dissimilar to the 'clouds' that fill out the space of the page in later forms of calligraphic exercises or in illuminated texts. These irregular filling elements or 'clouds' are decorated with abstract ornamental motifs, a peacock-eye pattern being most common, which was derived directly from the early polychrome lustre painted pottery of Samarra.

27. **Ceramic bowl with lustre-painted decoration from Cairo.** 12th century. diam. *c.* 12 in. (30·5 cm.). Museum of Islamic Art, Cairo. Fatimid painting survives mainly on lustre-painted pottery. The figurative style derives from Samarra painting. Although lively and realistic in detail, the subject-matter is often organised into formal, heraldic patterns.

28. **Painting from the ceiling of the Cappella Palatina, Palermo,** Sicily. Painted by Fatimid artists in 1142. This is one of numerous paintings on the wooden ceiling of the Cappella Palatina. There are also many scenes of court life in which the symbolisme and decorative motifs are equally typical of Roger's Sicily, Frederic's Aqulia, Fatimid Egypt, or Abbasid Iraq. The Cappella Palatina paintings are, in fact, eloquent proof of the cultural unity of the Mediterranean region in the 12th century.

29. **Two panels from a casket with carved decoration.**
Ivory. 12th century. Egypt. *c.* 10 × 2½ in. (25 × 6·4 cm.).
Staatliche Museen zu Berlin. Entirely Abbasid in tradition, the
figures of musicians and hunters on these small ivory panels

demonstrate once more the importance of cultural contacts
between the Fatimid and the Abbasid courts. The figures have a
remarkable freedom of movement, the faces an intense
individuality.

The second style is probably largely dependent on a tradition of book painting developed in Iraq and Syria from hellenistic models. Nothing of the contemporary painting of this type is known directly, as the earliest surviving manuscripts made in Baghdad and in Syria date only from the early 13th century. These, however, undoubtedly follow a tradition first established in the 9th and 10th centuries. At any rate a school of Islamic hellenistic painting must have existed in Egypt in the 12th century because of the appearance of this second style in Fatimid lustre pottery.

It is characterised by a general movement away from traditional Iraqi iconography and by a new interest in everyday life. The pottery bowls are usually decorated with elaborate and very lively scenes, with groups of people engaged in various activities: carrying loads, wrestling, working, conversing or fighting, etc. The figures in these scenes are drawn in a sketchy, at times almost impressionistic manner and there is no heavy, defining outline. There are few decorative details in the background and secondary motifs are rare. The most striking feature, apart from the obviously different pictorial tradition, is the great realism and direct observation suggested by the everyday subject-matter. This pottery is of interest in that it preserves a style of figurative representation which gives us a good idea of what the wall and book painting of the Fatimid court school in Cairo must have been like, although no actual examples survive.

Fatimid painting seems to have rivalled the painting of the court in Baghdad and a report of a competition between an Iraqi and an Egyptian painter, in the middle of the 11th century has survived. At the invitation of Yazuri, the Vizir of the Fatimid caliph al-Mustansir, the two painters were asked to represent a dancing girl in a niche in a wall in such a way as to make her appear either coming out of a

doorway or entering it. The problem was solved by both painters in the same fashion, that is through a skilful use of colour, contrasting the colour of the girl's dress with that of the background. The Egyptian painter won. The story demonstrates the high esteem in which painting was held at the Fatimid court and it shows that there was apparently no difference in style between Baghdad and Cairo at the time—a fact amply borne out by the painting on pottery.

The painting on the ceiling of the Cappella Palatina, the chapel in Roger II of Sicily's palace which was completed in 1140, are in most important details identical to the style of Samarra. They must have been executed by Fatimid painters whom Roger II had brought to Sicily. Among the great many scenes of courtly life in the Cappella Palatina paintings, we find all the typical features of Iraqi tradition. The ruler is represented frontally with his ceremonial wine cup in his left hand, flanked by attendants. All have full round faces with enormous almond-shaped eyes, and all are shown frontally in the late classical manner, inherited from the Central Asian hellenistic tradition.

CARVING AND THE 'INFINITE PATTERN'

Some other forms of Fatimid art are equally indebted to the Abbasid tradition. Wood and ivory carvings, for example, which were produced in large numbers and were of high quality, followed a tradition already established under the Tulunids, the iconography being derived almost exclusively from Abbasid court art.

At the same time a form of abstract ornamentation of larger surfaces was developed which was to become one of the most successful forms of abstract Islamic art. Based on the simple principle of infinite systems of linear patterns that, being superimposed one upon another, create geometrical forms, stars, polygons, and triangles, these designs for the first time developed fully the most fundamental of

30. Mihrab from the Mausoleum of Sayyiddah Rukhaiyah. 1154–1160. Wood. 82¾ × 43¾ in. (210 × 111 cm.). Museum of Islamic Art, Cairo. While the floral and figurative elements in Fatimid art were very realistic, a style of linear abstraction was also developed that found its strongest expression in the decoration of wooden objects for religious buildings: minbars, mihrabs, doors, kursis, etc. This mihrab is one of the best preserved examples of a style that has a long history in Western Islamic art, reaching Seljuk Anatolia and the Atabek territories, and finally, after the 13th century, all parts of the Muslim world.

31. Bronze figure of a griffin, Egypt. 11th–12th century. *c.* 59 in. (150 cm.). Campo Santo, Pisa. Animal sculpture, rare in Islamic art, seems to have been developed first in Umayyad Spain and Fatimid Egypt. The Pisa Griffin is outstanding for its highly decorative ornamental detail and the beautifully sensitive shape of the animal's body. Bronze sculptures like this probably served as models in Seljuk Iran for similar but generally much smaller sculptures in the later 12th and 13th centuries. Many Fatimid craftsmen migrated to Iran after the fall of the Fatimid dynasty in 1171.

all Islamic design concepts, that of the infinite pattern. The infinite pattern becomes so much a part of all Islamic art that one easily overlooks the fact that it was not created accidentally out of a general desire for abstraction or to solve the 'dilemma of a basically iconoclastic civilisation' as Islamic civilisation has often been wrongly interpreted. That figurative art existed at all times in Islamic art is by now self-evident. But it was in the same Fatimid period, so rich and varied in its figurative art, that the abstract linear pattern was developed, being used particularly for stone carving, architectural decoration, and the woodcarving of *30* mihrabs, minbars and doors, which could just as easily have been decorated with figurative scenes as are the tie-beams of the western Fatimid palace, which are entirely decorated with court scenes and animals. The Fatimid woodcarver excelled equally in the design of floral patterns and arabesque compositions that often continue directly the earlier Samarra tradition.

OTHER DECORATIVE ARTS

Of the decorative arts little besides pottery has come down to us. The treasures of the Fatimids must have been extraordinary and they have been extensively described. Gold objects and precious stones and jewellery seem to have existed in great quantities, and the few surviving magnificent wood and ivory carvings as well as some crystal cups and ewers that were made in Cairo in the 10th and 11th centuries demonstrate the high level of the arts and crafts of the Fatimid capital.

Of Fatimid metalwork very little seems to have survived,

33 (right). **Glass beaker with cut relief decoration from Egypt.** 12th century. h. *c.* 5 in. (12·7 cm.). Veste Coburg Collection, Northern Bavaria. The best example of cut glass to have survived, this beaker imitates the more difficult technique of rock crystal carving. With its powerfully angled cutting it comes amazingly close to achieving the effect of cut crystal.

32. **Rock crystal ewer from Cairo,** Egypt. 10th century. Inscribed with the name of the Fatimid Caliph Al-Azis Billah (975–96) h. 7 1/16 in. (18 cm.). Tesoro di San Marco, Venice. This magnificent ewer is generally considered to be the masterpiece of a small group of pear-shaped rock crystal ewers with carved low relief decoration. As the inscription makes clear, it was made for the ruler himself and must have been fashioned by one of the leading masters of the royal workshops in Cairo.

apart from a few small bowls and ewers. All the more striking, therefore, are a number of cast bronze animal figures of which the most impressive is of monumental size and superb workmanship. The large griffin in the Camposanto *31* in Pisa is probably one of the most ambitious pieces of cast metal ever produced by Muslim artists.

Rock crystal carvings seem to have been produced already in Tulunid times but the pieces that can safely be ascribed to that period are all small in scale and show purely abstract arabesque patterns in low relief. With the general development of a figurative style in the Fatimid period rock crystal beakers and ewers were decorated with *32, 33* a variety of animal groups among delicately designed arabesques. Some of these pieces are of exquisite workmanship and superb design. These objects were so much esteemed in the Muslim world that they gave rise to a school of cut glass in Iran that imitated, often quite successfully, the special effect of the carved rock crystal.

Embroidery and tapestry work of exquisite quality were **13** made in Egypt at this time, employing mainly abstract patterns, using much gold, and some red. The most attractive examples are those that follow again the general line of figurative iconography.

Under the Fatimids the highest point in western Islamic art was reached, combining a variety of different traditions in a unique way only rivalled in the West by Spain. In the use of architectural forms both of the classical decorative and eastern (Iraqi) tradition, and in the application of classical decorative and eastern Islamic figurative forms to every kind of surface, the Fatimids created an art that in its beauty and interest is outstanding in the whole history of Islam.

The Art of the Seljuk Turks in Iran

Among the many local dynasties that had established themselves in the eastern part of the Muslim empire and gained more and more strength and importance as the central power of the caliphate declined, the Seljuk Turks, one of the groups of Turkish peoples that had migrated into Iran with the Ghuzz tribes of Central Asia, gained superiority and finally control of Iran in the middle of the 11th century, wresting control from the Buyids. Nominally protectors of the caliph in Baghdad, the Seljuks created an independent kingdom in Persia. During their reign, which lasted until the Mongol conquest in the early 13th century, Iran saw its highest form of cultural development in Islamic times. The art of the Seljuk Turks, who took over Anatolia in the 12th century, dominated most of the Muslim world in the 12th and 13th centuries.

ARCHITECTURE

The Seljuks were great builders. During their reign a number of classical architectural forms were established which persisted in Iran practically into modern times. Earlier Iranian mosques had followed the Arab model, but this plan was now changed in accord with the ancient Iranian tradition to a four-ivan court mosque, introducing the ivan-hall and dome chamber design of pre-Islamic Iranian palatial architecture. In the centre of each side of the courtyard a large ivan-hall is inserted that interrupts the two-storey running arcades. The prayer hall ivan, often considerably larger than those of the other three sides, runs into a square dome chamber in front of the mihrab emphasising the kibla. F

The most important surviving mosque of this type is the Masjid-i Jami in Isfahan, built by order of Malik Shah (1072–92). Massive ivan-halls appear in the centre of the long sides, with a long, tall ivan-hall behind the entrance. Opposite it at the far end of the large court is the huge prayer hall ivan and dome chamber. Inside the enormous dome that surmounts the high, square chamber is an inscription in Kufic characters carried out in brick showing Malik Shah's name. Above the chamber itself are ingenious rows of blind niches with pointed arches which transform the square into the circle of the dome. This becomes the standard design for the intermediary zone and appears 34 35

34. **Dome of Malik Shah, Masjid-i Jami, Isfahan, Iran,** 1080. The Masjid-i Jami of Isfahan is probably the major monument of Seljuk architecture in Iran. Although not the earliest building of its kind, it is certainly the most sumptuous and monumental, and provides a model for almost all later mosque buildings in Iran. The main dome, above the chamber in the prayer hall in front of the mihrab, was raised by order of Malik Shah in 1080. Its classical form, pure and perfect in outline and devoid any decoration, is testimony to the particular concept of architectural form developed by the Seljuks in Iran.

with variations in all major buildings of the period. The new features exemplified in this building were later to serve as models for Mongol architecture.

The Seljuks developed a great number of architectural forms, notably the religious school complex (madrasah). This consisted of an open court surrounded by rooms, small ivan-halls that served as class-rooms, and often a domed chamber mosque on one side. Many tomb towers and shrines were built and numerous monumental mosques of which only a few survive intact, either because they were destroyed or because they were modified at later periods. The great mosques of Ardistan, Gulpayagan and Kazvin (Qazvin) still retain large parts of their original form, particularly the kibla-ivan-dome-chamber sequence.

ARCHITECTURAL DECORATION

Architectural decoration reached an especially high level. Although plasterwork, decorative brick-laying, or applied brick patterns had been used before, especially in Central Asia, it was only in the Seljuk period that these techniques, especially plaster decoration, were used on a monumental scale in Iran. Large surfaces of architectural structures are coated with plaster into which ornament is cut or moulded, and entire mihrabs are made out of plaster with elegantly designed inscriptions, frames and cornices, border bands, and magnificent floral filler ornament.

The most important of all architectural decoration developed in Seljuk times is the use of glazed brick- and tile-work. The lustre-painted tiles of Kashan, the main centre of pottery in the 12th and 13th centuries, were the result of centuries of experimentation. It may be remembered that in the Jausak al-Khakani palace in Samarra, lustre-painted tiles were used for wall decoration. But while there the polychrome and pictorial aspect of the tiles was still dominant, in the lustre tiles of Kashan a complete fusion between pictorial art and architectural effect was achieved. Lustre-painting with its extraordinary sheen outstrips any other medium of architectural decoration in its ability to dissolve the solid masses of architectural structures. Only lustre can create a complete optical illusion of insubstantiality. In reflecting light and making the surface of a wall shine like glass or gold, the effect of lustre-painted tiles is virtually to dissolve the matter that carries it—clay, mortar, brick and stone.

POTTERY AND PAINTING

Although important schools of pottery had previously been developed in Abbasid Iraq, Samanid Khurassan and Central Asia, and Fatimid Egypt, it was only in Seljuk Iran that pottery became a major art-form. Many different types were developed using highly sophisticated techniques. Among these the most important, as in architectural decoration, is that of lustre-painting. The technique was almost certainly imported from Egypt, from where Cairo potters had migrated in large numbers to the Seljuk court in Rayy in search of new employment after the fall of the

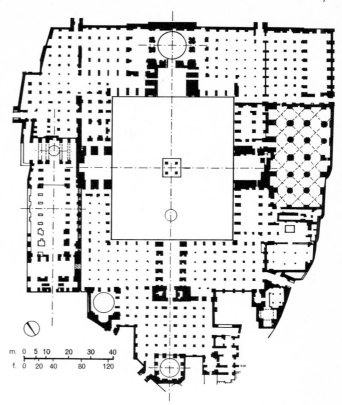

m. 0 5 10   20   30   40
f. 0   20   40   80   120

F. Plan of the Masjid-i Jami, Isfahan.

35. **View of the squinch in Malik Shah's dome chamber** in the Masjid-i Jami, Isfahan, Iran. 1080. This view, showing the link between the square plan of the dome chamber and the circle of the dome, taken from directly below the corner squinch, shows clearly the ingenious and complex way in which the problem of transition was solved. This form of squinch becomes standard in all later Iranian architecture.

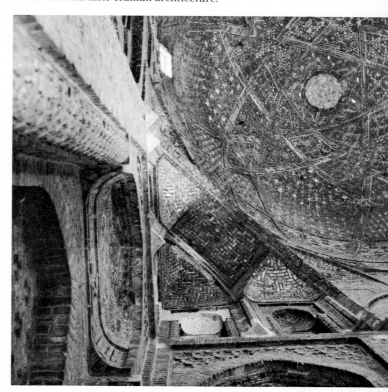

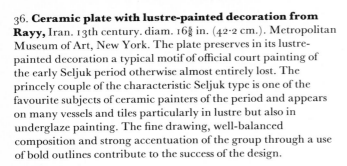

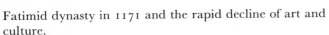

36. **Ceramic plate with lustre-painted decoration from Rayy,** Iran. 13th century. diam. 16⅝ in. (42·2 cm.). Metropolitan Museum of Art, New York. The plate preserves in its lustre-painted decoration a typical motif of official court painting of the early Seljuk period otherwise almost entirely lost. The princely couple of the characteristic Seljuk type is one of the favourite subjects of ceramic painters of the period and appears on many vessels and tiles particularly in lustre but also in underglaze painting. The fine drawing, well-balanced composition and strong accentuation of the group through a use of bold outlines contribute to the success of the design.

37. **Ceramic bowl with carved design from Iran.** First half 12th century. diam. 6½ in. (16·5 cm.). Victoria and Albert Museum, London. Among the many monochrome glazed wares produced in the Seljuk period in Iran those with pure white surfaces are undoubtedly the most beautiful. With the carving and moulding of the ceramic body a very light relief pattern was created on the surface of the vessels, usually of a highly abstract character but almost always deriving from some plant form.

Fatimid dynasty in 1171 and the rapid decline of art and culture.

With their arrival, pottery making in the East changed completely. They not only brought the secret of lustre-painting; they also taught the Persians to make a new artificial ceramic body of quartz and other glassy matters, very similar to the material from which the glazes themselves were made. This created a much closer bond between body and glaze. Alkaline glazes, so far unknown in Iran, were also developed and made true under-glaze painting possible.

36 Most important and most immediately derived from Fatimid Egypt is the lustre style of Rayy, near Teheran. The same Fatimid concept of figurative decoration against a solid lustre ground is found at Rayy. There is a clear contrast between light and dark, decorated and un-decorated areas, a conscious division between motif and background. The pictorial style obviously developed under the direct supervision of the Seljuk Turks. Facial features are entirely un-Iranian. The people represented are Central Asian Turks, such as are encountered for the first time in the 6th- and 7th-century paintings of Manichaean Turks in the Turfan area.

There are court scenes—princes and ladies of the royal household in gardens (shown by simple floral scrolls), horsemen hunting with falcons, playing polo or in battle. Some pieces are decorated with small-scale arabesque patterns or animal friezes in lustre on a white ground.

Bowls of various shapes, plates, small ewers, bottle-shaped vases, and jugs range from thick, heavy ones to fine and delicate pieces. A large, flat, narrow rimmed heavy plate is quite common, usually decorated with large figures or animals with the outside often glazed a deep cobalt blue. Another typical shape is a small thin-walled light bowl with a narrow base and steep, slightly curved sides. Such pieces are often decorated with a single seated figure, or a series of small figures around the rim and a small group in the centre.

Tiles were also made in Rayy and although monochrome glazed tiles of a magnificently brilliant turquoise blue are more common, lustre tiles have survived in considerable numbers.

The second lustre style of the Seljuk period was that of the workshops of Kashan, especially famous for lustre-painted tiles, decorated both with abstract floral and figurative designs, and known as *kashis* or *kashanis*. Many major buildings were decorated with kashanis, and mih-rabs were made from moulded, glazed and lustre-painted tile panels. The Kashan lustre style is of a peculiar and un-mistakable nature. All elements of the design form one intricate pattern creating an all-over, uniform effect. The background behind the floral, animal, or human forms is usually covered with solid lustre which is in turn decorated with dense incised patterns of fine spirals or short, curved lines and dots that break up the solidity of the brown lustre. Then every part of the actual design against this lustre

38. Ceramic vase with moulded relief design from Iran. 13th century. h. 25¾ in. (65·4 cm.). Freer Gallery of Art, Washington. Large pieces of pottery are uncommon in Islamic art and it was only during the Seljuk period in Iran that elaborately decorated pieces, combining relief moulding, monochrome glazing, painting and gilding, were produced. This piece is notable for the figures which appear in the relief decoration.

39. Head of a Seljuk Prince. Part of a statue of stucco. Iran, 12th century. h. 10 in. (25·4 cm.). Metropolitan Museum of Art, New York. Sculpture in the round is rare in Islamic art either in the East or West. In this portrait of a Seljuk prince a facial type can be recognised that was to become characteristic of Eastern Islamic art throughout the 12th and 13th centuries. Although highly stylised, it is undoubtedly based on the typical physical features of the ruling class—the Seljuk Turks.

background is covered with similar patterns, painted in lustre so densely and minutely that a distinction between background and object is often difficult. Only the faces of the groups of human figures remain as small, clear white areas within the all-over design. Many tiles and vessels decorated in this style are inscribed and dated, unusual in medieval Islamic pottery. Kashan lustre ware continues into the 14th century and carries a major Seljuk tradition into the Mongol period.

Among many Seljuk ceramic wares that cannot with certainty be attributed to any one pottery centre, the so-called *minai* ware deserves special attention. This very fine, delicate ware is one of the most beautiful types of Islamic pottery. A polychrome, overglaze painted pottery, it seems to have been made throughout the 12th and 13th centuries. The style and subject-matter of its predominantly figurative decoration reflect the otherwise almost entirely lost art of Seljuk book and wall-painting. The variety of shapes of the usually small and carefully made pieces, little bowls, ewers, cups, vases, bottles, and plates, is amazing. Equally varied are the brilliant colours, set off against an either buff white or blue background. The richness of iconographic detail is impressive evidence of a strong trend towards

figurative expression in Eastern Islamic art. Although most minai pieces are small, a few monumental pieces exist. Among them the large plate in the Freer Gallery in Washington is undoubtedly the most important. Its unique decoration, an elaborate battle scene showing the siege of a city by a large army led by a cavalcade of horsemen, is probably taken from a wall-painting in the royal palace, famous in its time. The reverse side has a large-scale group of huntsmen in a forest and a variety of real and fantastic animals. The facial type is again that of the Central Asian Turks. The same slanting eyes, straight noses, minute mouths in full round faces, the same long, black hair falling in full tresses on their shoulders.

Only a single manuscript of this school of painting and a few fragmentary wall-paintings have survived. The manuscript of the *Warkah wa Gulshah* poem in Istanbul is undated and gives no indication of where it was made, except for the mention of the painter's name with a nisbah (usually considered to show the origin of a person, but frequently also a reference to a person's residence) that points to Eastern Anatolia. The style of the paintings that illustrate this text leave, however, no doubt as to its origin in the 12th-century Seljuk territory.

40. **Brass cup-bowl with silver inlay design,** the 'Wade Cup' from Iran. Early 13th century. diam. 6⅜ in. (16·5 cm.). h. 4½ in. (10·5 cm.). Museum of Art, Cleveland. One of a group of high stem cup-bowls, this piece is especially interesting because of its unusually elaborate figurative rendering of the inscription around the rim, and the intricate zodiacal patterning of the small diamond-shaped fields formed by an interlace band running over the body. The transformation of calligraphic forms into figurative decoration seems first to have been developed in the 12th century on metalwork in Central Asia and Khurassan from where it spread to the rest of Iran.

The paintings in the manuscript follow the same principle as those on minai pottery. Tightly packed scenes full of action and with many small figures engaged in battle or argument; few scenes have single figures and then they are almost always imbedded into a solidly coloured background or complex architectural framework. Only rarely do single figures or single objects stand alone in open, uncluttered space. Although this is a romantic-poetical text and does not really call for the inclusion of any royal iconography, there are scenes that give glimpses of that part of Seljuk pictorial art.

Scenes of court life and the royal entourage abound, however, on minai pottery which often recalls book illustration. A famous piece is a small beaker in Washington with scenes from the *Shah-nameh*. There are bowls with scenes showing Bahram Gur hunting, Dahhak being led away, single scenes from Firdusi's poem, which seems to have been a popular subject.

Possibly by the middle of the century a polychrome overglaze painted pottery was developed known as *Lajvardina* ware, easily identified by its deep cobalt blue background painted with abstract linear and floral designs in gold and red. This ware persists into the 14th century and belongs technically speaking to the Mongol period but so many

Seljuk art forms continued into the post-Seljuk period that strict divisions are difficult.

The pottery decorated with incised and carved design is extremely accomplished and has figurative decoration—mainly animal motifs—of the finest quality. Its balanced linear incised design is also seen in Seljuk metalwork. A particular type using carved, incised or moulded relief motifs, and specialising in monochrome glazes is of great beauty and interest. Brilliant turquoise blue, deep cobalt blue, an purplish colour of various shades, and white are the principle colours. Sometimes different colour glazes are used together, predominantly cobalt blue and white, white being the main colour, with details picked out in blue. The incised designs are largely abstract-floral. They often penetrate so deeply that they pierce the thickness of the walls of a bowl or a ewer. In some cases, small holes are pierced along the outlines of designs or all over the background. These minute openings are filled by the heavily running glaze and remain translucent when held against the light giving an appearance of translucency which the pottery does not actually have. With this technique the quality of the Chinese porcelain which could not be made in the Islamic world because of the lack of kaolin clay was imitated. It continued in use throughout the history of Islamic

37

41. **Engraved silver plate from Iran.** Made by Hasan al-Kashani for Sultan Alp Arslan in AH 459 (1066 AD). Diam. 17 in. (43·2 cm.). Museum of Fine Arts, Boston. This large silver platter, engraved with an elaborate arabesque and animal design above and below the bold inscription in the centre, is inscribed with the name of Sultan Alp Arslan (1063–1072) the second of the great Seljuk rulers of Iran. With a silver candlestick in the same collection it comprises a most important group of silverwork from the early Islamic period in the East.

pottery still being employed for 17th-century Persian white wares.

Among the moulded wares a group of monumental pieces stand out. These are very tall vases moulded in various registers in various degrees of relief and glazed either in deep cobalt or light turquoise blue. The most magnificent piece is again in the collection of the Freer Gallery in Washington and excels not only in a very high relief and perfect modelling of the individual features but also in the fact that its decoration is largely figurative. The entire surface seems furthermore to have been gilded. Other vases and moulded ware all share the stylistic features of Kashan.

A variety of other ceramic wares was produced in Seljuk Iran which, on the evidence of a unique medieval text describing the Kashan workshops, can also be attributed to that city. The most important ware has figurative patterns painted in black under a turquoise glaze. Many pieces are very similar to lustre-painted ware but some are extraordinary examples of the extremely difficult technique of openwork. They have a double shell, the inner one serving as the actual container while the outer one is pierced and cut out in a fashion that is more like metalwork than pottery.

SCULPTURE

Sculpture is generally rare in Islamic art, especially sculpture in the full round. But some of the stucco sculptures that survive from the destroyed palaces of Rayy come close to monumental proportions and are in part, particularly in the heads of human figures, worked almost in the full round, even though the figures always remain attached to the wall. Sculptural forms in the true sense have been developed, however, in other media, notably pottery and metalwork, and to a lesser degree in glass and ivory. A large number of pottery figurines survive which date mainly from the 12th and early 13th centuries. Many are hollow and serve utilitarian functions such as jugs, vases, or candlesticks, but others are made of solid clay, glazed in deep cobalt or light turquoise blue, with painted under-glaze or lustre, and modelled often with great sensitivity for their human or animal form. These objects are truly small sculptures, some continuing a formal tradition that reaches far back into pre-Islamic times.

METALWORK

The most important element of Seljuk metalwork, the enrichment of the metal surface, bronze or brass, through silver inlay, goes back to pre-Seljuk times, although it was

never developed very far before the 12th century. Early bronzes, of which a good number survive, have only engraved designs, usually limited to a few inscriptions, *41* floral scrolls and arabesque patterns.

The most famous among the early silver inlaid metal pieces is the so-called Bobrinski bucket in the Hermitage **14** made by Muhammad ibn Abd al-Wahid and Masud ibn Ahmad in Herat in 1163 for a rich merchant. This bucket closely follows earlier pieces in shape and general treatment *42* but it has abandoned the simple form of engraved decoration for an elaborate design in silver inlay at once abstract, calligraphic and figurative. This is the first silver inlaid piece that can with certainty be associated with a bourgeois milieu. Although largely following court iconography in its figurative decoration—drinking, hunting, and sporting scenes—it is not made for a prince or a noble of the realm but for a man who in his new wealth obviously attempted to imitate the grandeur and leisure of courtly life. The object is therefore doubly interesting and a perfect example of the taste and style of the day.

Seljuk artists created a number of impressive sculptures in bronze. Most of these pieces are aquamaniles or incense burners—utility objects, but with such a perfection of line and balance of shape in arrested movement that they may truly be called sculpture. They are usually decorated with fine incised patterns of semi-abstract floral nature, and in some instances bodies of feline animals or birds which are *43* perforated, again with floral patterns, forming a kind of lacework through which the incense could escape. Such an object in action must have been one of the most perfect realisations of the Islamic ideal of dissolving matter through artistic means.

42. **Bronze bucket from Iran.** Made by Muhammad ibn Nasir ibn Muhammad al-Harawi. 12th century. h. *c.* 10 in. (25·5 cm.). Hermitage, Leningrad. This bucket is closely related in shape to the more famous Bobrinski Bucket but different in its unusual organisation of the surface into rectangular panels alternately filled with interlace band motifs and star-rosettes surrounded by animals. It is an excellent example of the flourishing school of metalwork in Khurassan. Highly original in its general design and individual detail, the piece demonstrates the various possibilities in metal design in the early Seljuk period.

43. **Incense burner in form of a cat.** Made by Jafar ibn Muhammad ibn Ali in 1181. Bronze with openwork decoration and engraving. h. 33½ in. (85·1 cm.). Metropolitan Museum of Art, New York. This Seljuk bronze incense burner is unusual both in its size and its quality. It can best be compared with the Fatimid bronze griffin in Pisa (figure 31). The extraordinary ornamentation of the animal's body which is entirely perforated in an elaborate palmette design, contributes to the dematerialising effect that the general ornamentation of the bronze surface is obviously meant to achieve. Generally thought to be of Iranian workmanship, it may be that the piece was actually made in Iraq or Syria.

The period of Seljuk rule in Iran (and Anatolia) is probably the most important of early Islamic culture. Fundamental forms of architectural design are developed and permanently formulated for later periods. The most important are the four-ivan court mosque, and the madrasah on a similar plan—also standard forms for tomb towers and square-plan domed mausolea, which, although going back to pre-Seljuk times, are fixed in their traditional designs for Eastern Islam only in the 11th century under the Seljuk Turks.

An enormous expansion of figurative representation and the development of an iconography based on Central Asian models, resulting in the creation of a special representational type for the ruler's image and another for the ruling class, is probably the most interesting achievement of the period. A vast territory, stretching from Central Asia to the Bosporus and the centre of Syria, is united in one culture that dominated both eastern and western Islam for at least a century after the downfall of the Seljuk rulers in Iran.

The Art of the Seljuk Turks in Anatolia

Anatolia was conquered by the Seljuk Turks and an independent dynasty established in 1078 with Sulayman ibn Kutlumish (1078–86) who became governor after the battle of Manzikert in which the Byzantines were decisively defeated. Konya in Central Anatolia became the capital during the reign of Masud I (1116–56). It was during the 13th century under the rule of Kay Khusrau and his successors, Izz al-din Kay Kaus I and Ala al-din (Alaeddin) Kay Kubad, that the Seljuk culture flourished in Anatolia reaching its peak in the mid-century when the Seljuks of Iran had already been annihilated by Chingiz Khan and those of Anatolia were engaged in a losing battle against the invading Mongols.

After the defeat of Kay Khusrau II's army in 1242, the Seljuks became vassals of the Mongol ruler of Iran. The result was a rapid decline of Seljuk power in Anatolia and the eventual collapse of a central government. Turkoman invasions and internal struggle weakened the realm and after a period of anarchy, the Seljuk line became extinct at the beginning of the 14th century.

Seljuk art in Anatolia, although closely related to that of Seljuk Iran, developed a very definite character of its own. Different forms of mosque, madrasah and *türbe* (tomb tower) were created and the *caravansarayi*—a resthouse for caravans and their entourage—was fully developed. Techniques and forms of architectural decoration were introduced that number among the most original and successful in Islamic art and were of great significance for the further development of western Islamic art and architecture. Much of the difference between Seljuk art in Anatolia and in Iran stems from the different cultural traditions in Anatolia. Byzantine and Armenian stone architecture provided the new rulers with a wealth of models and ideas and the country was rich in building materials. Much therefore survives of Seljuk architecture in Anatolia while little survives in Iran. But the pictorial tradition, judging from the exceedingly scanty remains, seems to have been identical and other art forms, such as lustre-painted and polychrome over-glaze painted tilework, also testify to the basic cultural unity of both regions in the 12th and 13th centuries.

ARCHITECTURE

The court-ivan mosque does not seem to have been favoured in Anatolia. The majority of surviving mosques have no court and focus on a multiple support prayer hall with one or more domes at the kibla wall. This domed area is not closed off as in the Seljuk mosques of Iran but forms an integral part of the design. From this the unified central dome of the Ottoman Turkish mosque develops.

In the Alaeddin Cami in Nigde (1223) three domes are placed at the kibla wall, corresponding to the three aisles of the prayer hall. In the Ulu Cami in Divrigi (1228–29) a single dome with a pointed tent roof on the outside appears in front of the mihrab at the end of the central aisle, slightly wider than the double aisles on either side. An important feature of these buildings is also that they are more often organised in a longitudinal direction rather than in the traditional lateral direction of the Arab mosque.

The Alaeddin Cami in Konya, founded by Rukhn al-din Mazud (1116–56) but with modifications by subsequent rulers, consists of an irregular enclosure with an irregularly shaped prayer hall to the south and a court to the north. In front of a smaller prayer hall to the west, probably the oldest part of the building, (between 1156–92), appear two polygonal türbes, of which one is the sultan's mausoleum. This smaller prayer hall has a dome chamber tract that recalls somewhat Seljuk designs in Iran but the square room in front of the dome does not open in the form of an ivan to the court but to a long lateral aisle along the entire prayer hall. The prayer hall is closed to the court—a later addition—and actually separated from it by the türbes. The entire eastern part of the mosque, its large prayer hall with eleven aisles running parallel to the kibla wall and a court which again does not communicate with the prayer hall belong to the final building period of Alaeddin. Even though there are a court and a prayer hall in this design, their relationship is of an entirely different nature from that of the Arab or the Seljuk mosque in Iran. The court becomes a kind of atrium or plaza in front of the closed mosque and even though domed rooms are included there is no access to them from the court. An imposing entrance to the court becomes pointless and disappears, and instead there is a general elaboration of the exterior of the building with façades and gateways. This did not happen in Iran but was widespread in Seljuk Anatolia.

There are two types of madrasah in Seljuk Anatolia: the open court madrasah, as known in Iran, Iraq and western Islam, and the closed dome chamber madrasah, which seems to be a Seljuk development in Anatolia. The latter type dominates among the surviving 13th-century buildings, although major examples of the open court four-ivan madrasah also exist.

Of the dome chamber madrasah, the Karatay Madrasah and the Ince Minare, both in Konya, are undoubtedly the most perfect, built on a simple square plan with a large central room, surmounted by a monumental dome and flanked by oblong rooms. Smaller corner dome chambers are placed at the rear right and left of an ivan-hall opening onto the central dome chamber. Both buildings excel in rich decoration with glazed brick and faience mosaic both outside and inside, and count among the most remarkable achievements of Seljuk architecture in Anatolia. The Karatay Madrasah, built by Celaleddin Karatay, grand vizir of Kay Kaus II, in 1251, has one of the finest surviving marble portals with marbles of different colours and precise, linear relief carving, while the Ince Minare, built by Fahr al-din Ali in 1258, has in its carved light-red stone façade one of the most unusual forms of epigraphic and plastic decoration.

A great variety of türbe buildings have survived in Anatolia, based on those of Seljuk Iran. Built on square,

21, 44
45

44. **Interior of the Dome of the Madrasah of Celaleddin Karatay Konya,** Turkey. 1251. The brilliant glazed brick and faience decoration of the Karatay Madrasah belongs to the finest ceramic architectural decoration in any age. The pattern of the dome interior, comprising very intricate interlacing band ornament producing, at certain points, staggered rows of 'bursting suns', together with the design of the squinches in the form of elongated triangles, also decorated with faience make this interior both delicate and astonishingly impressive.

polygonal or round plans, they are almost always vaulted by a shallow dome on the inside and a pointed tent roof on the outside, and decorated with fine stone carving, concentrated at the portal, the windows and the often elaborate corbel system that supports the overhanging roof. Türbes are known in Anatolia from the 12th century on and their form survives into the Ottoman period. A second specifically Anatolian type consists of an open ivan-hall. The actual tomb chamber is placed into an underground crypt, a feature common to all Seljuk türbes in Anatolia.

The caravansarayi was usually built on a single court plan surrounded by rooms serving obvious functions for man and animal. In Anatolia a special type was developed that had no parallel elsewhere. Even though there were Iranian caravansarayis of large or even monumental proportions, they were minor architectural works. The 13th-century Anatolian caravansarayi, however, is of great importance. It was usually very large, heavily fortified, with high, thick, well-constructed stone walls reinforced by bastion towers. A magnificent gate-structure led into a rectangular court; on the opposite side was a second gateway leading to an often monumental hall, comparable to medieval western European cathedral architecture. Divided into several aisles, the hall is covered by flat or pointed roofs supported by slender arches. The central aisle is raised and open to the sky in the middle.

These buildings obviously combine features of many different architectural designs, both religious and secular, but in their monumentality, solidity of construction and beauty of individual form and decoration they are among the masterpieces of Islamic architecture.

Of palatial architecture in Konya, Kubadabad and Diyar Bakr very little survives, but historical descriptions and recent excavations give some idea of their basic elements. They seem to combine traditional elements of ivan and dome chamber tracts for official reception and throne rooms, with a multitude of secondary rooms (the palace of Diyar Bakr is described as having fifty rooms) for the living quarters of the ruler and his entourage. A kiosk or pavilion from the palace of Alaeddin, Konya, which survived until early this century and finds of tilework and plaster suggest how richly the palaces were decorated. Polychrome stone and marble floors and mosaic decorations have been excavated on the site of Diyar Bakr and lustre-painted and black underglaze painted tilework both figurative and abstract has been found in the palace of Kubadabad.

The Seljuks of Anatolia were probably first to use coloured faience for architectural decoration on a monumental scale; tile mosaic and glazed bricks were only used in this way in Iran in Il-Khanid times. The style of tile and tile mosaic decoration developed in Konya in the 12th and 13th centuries was an inspiration for centuries to come, and was probably introduced to Iran from Anatolia.

Interiors of ivan-halls and domes, entire surfaces of walls, floors, portals, tombs, and even minarets were covered with glazed tiles, bricks, or combinations of both and finally with tile mosaic, using glazed clay plaques of different colours from which each individual form to be used in the design is cut. Leaves, letters, scrolls, flowers, and irregular shapes for background areas are pieced together in a clay and mortar bed directly onto the wall. This technique not only required consummate skill but much time and patience, an exceptional sense of design and the ability to organise a huge surface area. It also required an enormous supply of raw materials. The same technique was also used to construct mihrab niches. In short, although little Seljuk pottery has survived from Anatolia, there must have been large and active workshops to provide the builders with glazed tilework.

The main colours of these tiles and tile mosaics are blue, black and white, but there are also beautiful green tiles with black underglaze painted patterns or with patterns painted in gold on top of the glaze.

Tiles found in the ruins of the palace of Ala al-din in Konya also include overglaze painted polychrome ones of the minai type and it seems likely that minai ware in general was also produced in Anatolia.

Recent excavations of the palace in Kubadabad revealed a large number of star and cross-shaped tiles, mainly with figurative underglaze or lustre-painted decoration. Seated figures, animal groups and arabesque patterns, very much like 13th-century pottery in Iran and Syria (Rakka), dem-

45. **The Ince Minare Madrasah, Konya,** Turkey, 1258. This is the most famous of the dome-chamber madrasahs of Seljuk Anatolia. Its name derives from the particularly graceful minaret with blue glazed brick decoration, the upper part of which is now destroyed. The most interesting feature of the building is its portal which is decorated with a curious band ornament filled with inscriptions in low relief.

46. **Carved wooden lectern (rahle) from Turkey.** 13th century. Signed by Abd al-Wahid ibn Sulayman. w. 19¾ in. (50 cm.). h. 45½ in. (115·5 cm.). Staatliche Museen zu Berlin. Woodcarving became a major art form in Seljuk Anatolia. This lectern decorated with high relief arabesque scrolls is a typical example of the high quality of design and craftsmanship of the period. The fact that the piece is signed shows the importance of the wood-carver's craft at the time. The lectern would have been made either for a mosque or a madrasah and would therefore have been particularly carefully made.

47. **Metal door knocker from Iraq.** 12th century. Cast bronze with engraved design. l. 11 7/16 in. (29 cm.). Staatliche Museen zu Berlin. The motif of a dragon with a snake-like body and a tail ending in a griffin's head is quite common in Seljuk art in Anatolia, Syria and Iraq. Its special significance is not clear; it may have been heraldic, or it may have been cosmological-symbolical. This beautifully cast and unique bronze was very likely made in Iraq.

onstrate once more the cultural unity of the Seljuk-dominated part of the Muslim world.

Besides glazed tilework, simple brick patterns and moulded plaster relief were occasionally used, but the most important form of architectural decoration is stone-carving. Entire façades are covered with bands of inscriptions and floral and abstract linear patterns in various degrees of relief. At corners of buildings or at the base of minarets, and especially on entrance portals, the decoration is concentrated and sculptural. The most remarkable, if not altogether typical example is the gate of the Maristan in Divrigi where forms possibly originally conceived in plaster are translated into a unique sculptural stone-carving.

Among the finest Seljuk objects in Anatolia are the wood-carvings. Mihrabs, minbars and cenotaphs of large scale and intricate design are constructed of wood and decorated with inscriptions, abstract interlacing band ornament and floral motifs of a highly stylised nature. A great many of these objects are signed and dated, which shows the pride the woodcarvers took in their work.

KNOTTED RUGS

The earliest known knotted rugs are also from Seljuk Anatolia. The woollen knotted rug, one of the art forms most intimately associated with the Islamic world and its culture, was probably brought to western Asia by the Turkish tribes that entered the Muslim empire in the 8th and 9th centuries. It originated in an attempt to imitate animal furs by adding to a flat woven fabric additional woollen threads resembling the long hairs of animal fur. These were knotted into the weft and warp to reinforce it and give it additional thickness and volume. These artificial furs seem mainly to have been used as floor coverings in tents. It is impossible to say at which stage of its develop-

46

(Continued on page 97)

41. Ceramic plate from Syria.
12th–13th century. Incised design and
polychrome glaze. diam. 11⅛ in.
(25·7 cm.). Freer Gallery, Washington.
Incised designs appeared on Islamic
pottery from the very earliest periods, but
there is no evidence of figurative patterns
before the 12th century. The use of
different coloured glazes gives an added
liveliness of the design which has close
connections with a parallel tradition of
Byzantine ceramic decoration. There is a
close interrelationship between Islamic,
Byzantine, and Western European
ceramic decoration at this time.

**42. Enamelled glass bottle from
Aleppo, Syria.** 14th century. h. 15¾ in.
(40 cm.). Calouste Gulbenkian
Foundation Collection, Lisbon. This large
bottle, both in shape and in the colours
used in its decoration, is typical of
14th-century Syrian enamelwork.
Enamel-painted glass objects were
produced in great quantities from
the second half of the 13th century. The
decoration of this bottle, one of the finest
of the few pieces of equal size and richness
of decoration, consists of motifs of Chinese
inspiration, showing the strong cultural
influence of the Mongol civilisation
outside Iran. The kylin lion is taken
directly from Far Eastern iconography.

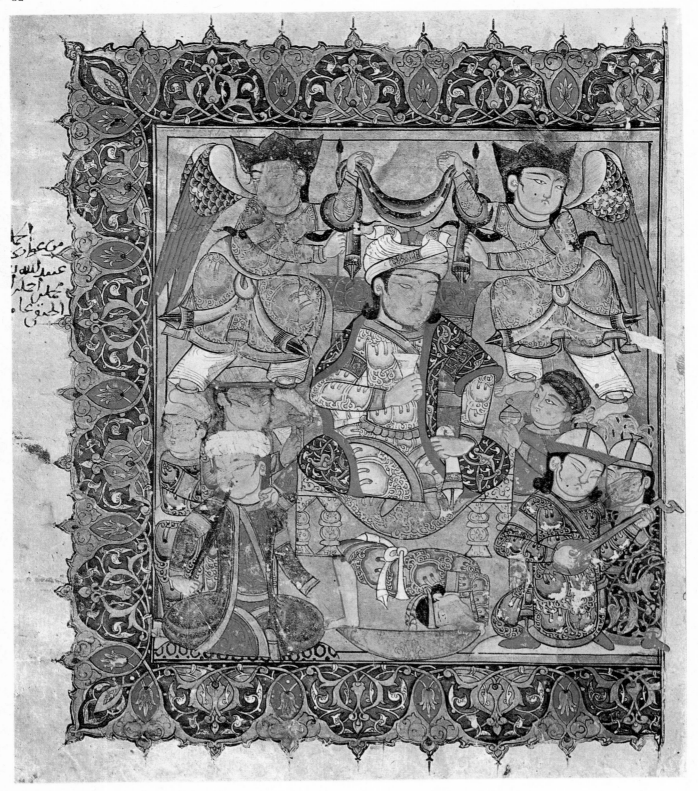

43. **Frontispiece painting from a copy of Hariri's Makamat** *(Assemblies)*. Egypt. 1334. $7\frac{5}{8} \times 6\frac{7}{8}$ in. (19·2 × 17·5 cm.). National Library, Vienna. This scene of royal entertainment shows the importance of Seljuk iconography in Mamluk painting. The ruler, seated cross-legged on his throne, holding the ceremonial beaker before him in his right hand, is a recurrent image in Eastern Islamic art from the 9th century onwards. Equally Seljuk in iconography is the cosmological symbol of a baldachin, derived from late classical Central Asian art, here represented by the cloth held over the ruler's head by angels.

44 (right). **Spanish carpet.** 15th century. 13 ft. 3 in. × 7 ft. 9 in. (4·2 × 2·4 m.). Museum of Art, Cleveland. Spanish carpets are a self-contained group. They employ a special technique, using a knot unknown elsewhere in carpet weaving, and possess original designs and colours, quite unequalled. This carpet, however, suggests a close contact with the Anatolian tradition. The octagonal medallions appear to derive almost directly from the so-called Holbein rugs. The curiously rigid organisation of the field into square compartments and the absence of a border are again typically Spanish features.

45. The Lion Court of the Alhambra Palace, Granada, Spain. 14th century. The Alhambra Palace, built by the Nasrid kings of Spain, is one of the most remarkable creations of Islamic architecture. The Lion Court in the centre of the Harim area, named after its fountain supported by stone figures of lions, is surrounded by arcades resting on alternating single and double columns of extraordinary elegance and lightness. The lion fountain has been said to be of earlier date, forming part of a 12th-century construction on the same site, but it is now generally accepted that it is contemporary with the Nasrid palace. Free-standing stone sculpture in the round is unusual in Islamic art.

46. **Entrance portal of the Masjid-i Jami, Kerman, Iran,** dated AH 750 1349 AD. The faience mosaic decoration of this mosque is one of the earliest examples of its kind in Iran. In its elaborate design and perfection of technique, it anticipates much of later Timurid architectural decoration in glazed brick and tilework.

47. **Mihrab of the Masjid-i Jami, Kerman, Iran.** 1349. The mihrab, occupying the whole end wall of the south-west ivan of the mosque is typical of faience mosaic decoration in mosque interiors in the Muzzaffarid period. This technique becomes of fundamental importance for Timurid architectural decoration in Iran. There is a marked contrast between precise geometric designs in an angular framework and freely-moving arabesque and scroll patterns. The brilliant colour, blue and white dominating, is the first step toward the superb polychromy of the 15th century.

48 (below). **Entrance to the Tomb of Tshutshuk Bika** (detail), Shah-i Zindeh, Samarkand. 1371. The decoration of the façade and entrance gate of the tomb is characteristic of the entire Shah-i Zindeh group. Glazed bricks, moulded relief and deep cut, polychrome glazed tilework are applied to the brick surface, covering it completely with a multiform abstract geometrical, arabesque and floral design, outstanding in its finesse and brilliance of colour. The idea of total tile revetment, developed for the first time in Central Asia towards the middle of the 14th century, becomes a standard feature of Timurid architecture.

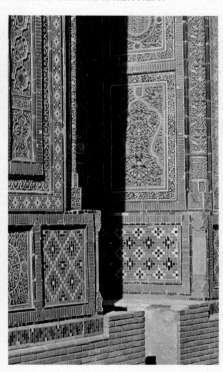

49. Gur-i Amir, Timur's Mausoleum, Samarkand. 1405. Originally planned as a mausoleum for Timur's nephew, Muhammad Sultan, who died in 1403, the building became the burial place of the ruling house. The emperor himself was buried here in 1405. Built on a polygonal exterior and square interior plan, with a double dome, the outer one being raised on a high drum, the mausoleum has features first developed in the Shah-i Zindeh (see plate 50). Unexpectedly it has a mosque-like façade. The magnificent decoration consists both of glazed brick and tilework and of carved marble.

50. **Shah-i Zindeh, the necropolis of the 'Living King',** near Samarkand. The Shah-i Zindeh consists of a group of sixteen tombs built around the tomb of Kasim ibn Abbas, a cousin of the Prophet, who had lived here venerated as a saint and as the 'Living King'. His tomb, as it appears today, was erected in 1334–5. The latest addition to the necropolis are the two tombs erected by Timur about 1400 for Oldsha Ain, his nurse, and Bibi Sineb, her daughter, seen in the foreground to the right. In 1434 Ulugh Beg, Timur's grandson, added a monumental portal to the complex.

53, 54. **Two paintings from a Timurid Anthology.** AH 813 (1410–11 AD). *Abraham's Sacrifice* and *Adam and Eve in Paradise*. Each 9¼ × 6¾ in. (23·5 × 14·6 cm.). Gulbenkian. Foundation Collection, Lisbon. This anthology was made for Shah Rukh's nephew, Iskandar, who lived in Shiraz where it is generally assumed to have been made. However, the Shiraz workshop was then using a totally different style and it is more likely that it was made at Herat, then sent to the prince, since the paintings are more in the tradition of late 14th-century Central Asia. They number among the finest produced in the Muslim East at that time.

55 (above). **Painting on silk from Herat.** *c.* 1400. 24¼ × 8 in. (61·5 × 20·5 cm.). Topkapi Sarayi Library, Istanbul. This painting belongs to a group preserved in an album forming one of the main works of the early Timurid style. The fine brushwork and the unusually mellow and subtle palette already anticipate the qualities of the Baysunghur workshop. The subject of the painting is not altogether clear but it might be an illustration for a text similar to the *Sulayman-nameh*. In fact, it could be that the princely couple carried by the servile monsters and accompanied by genii are Sulayman and the Queen of Sheba.

56 (below). **Painting in an album from Transoxiana or Herat.** *c.* 1400 9⅞ × 18⅞ in. (25 × 48 cm.). Topkapi Sarayi Library, Istanbul. This painting, possibly illustrating a story but more likely an assembly of various groups and figures out of different contexts is typical of the transitional style practised in Central Asia in the early Timurid period in its variety of different human types and the fine landscape consisting of a simple indication of rocky ground and shrubs. The different sources of inspiration were not yet fully assimilated but all the elements are already present that later appear in highly refined form in the first illustrated manuscripts that can be attributed to Herat.

57 (right). **Painting from a copy of Firdusi's Shah-nameh,** made for Baysunghur Mirza in Herat, AH 830 (1430 AD). *Isfandiyar slaying Arjasp in the Brazen Palace.* Page size 15 × 10¼ in. (38 × 26 cm.). Gulestan Palace Library, Teheran. The paintings in this manuscript are the main work of Baysunghur's workshop in Herat. This painting is unusual in the use of a complex architectural setting. Most notable is the contrast between static serenity and dramatic action, emphasised through the use of a curious system of quasi-perspective. The fine brushwork and the delicacy of both pattern and colour palette is also remarkable.

58 (above). **Painting from Mir
Haydar's Miraj-nameh,** copied and
illustrated in Herat in 1436. *The Prophet
Muhammad in Hell*. Page size 13½ × 14 in.
(34·3 × 35·5 cm.). Bibliothèque
Nationale, Paris. Painted after the death
of Baysunghur, the illustrations of this
unique manuscript continue the ideals of
the prince's workshop while on the other
hand a more immediate contact with the
pre-Baysunghur tradition of painting in
Herat and possibly Samarkand seems to
have been established. The subject,
depicting the various visions of the
Prophet on his *Night Journey through
Paradise and Hell*, is rare in Islamic
painting and constitutes one of the most
interesting cycles of religious painting.

59 (right). **Painting from a copy of
Nizami's Khamsa,** written in Herat,
AH 900. (1494–5 AD), painted by Abd
al-Razzak. *Muhammad's Ascension.*
8¼ × 5½ in. (21 × 14 cm.). British
Museum, London. A particularly
splendid example of the Prophet's
Night Journey. Although following a
well-established iconography,
Abd al-Razzak, who collaborated with
Mirak-nakkash and Bihzad on this
manuscript, has created an especially
brilliant design in the large golden cloud
bands that surround the Prophet. The
immediate influence of Central Asian
models for the cloud forms is noteworthy,
demonstrating the close contact between
Central Asia and the Herat school
throughout the 15th century.

**60. Ceramic plate from Northern
Iran.** Second half 15th century. Kubachi
style. Black underglaze painted
decoration. diam. 14¼ in. (36 cm.).
Victoria and Albert Museum, London.
Very little Timurid pottery has survived;
it seems that tilework absorbed most of the
energies of potters during the earlier part
of the 15th century. From later in the
century, however, some blue and black
underglaze painted pottery survives
from Kubachi, a small village in the
Caucasus. The strict limitation to two
colours and the exclusive use of purely
abstract decorative and epigraphic
motifs are typical of this ware.

61. Timurid gold ring with jade
seal-stone. Herat. *c.* 1430. diam. 1 in.
(2·5 cm.). Metropolitan Museum of Art,
New York. Surviving precious metal
objects are exceedingly rare in Islamic art
for they were easily destroyed. The
dragon motif was particularly popular
and jade carvings and bronze ewers with
dragon-headed handles that can be dated
and attributed through inscriptions to the
Timurid period and Central Asia,
survive in appreciable numbers.

48. Steel mirror from Turkey, with relief and gold inlay decoration. 13th century. diam. 8¼ in. (21 cm.). l. (complete with handle) 16¼ in. (41·5 cm.). Topkapi Sarayi Museum, Istanbul. The central medallion of this mirror is decorated with a scene from the courtly life of the Seljuk period: a hunter on horseback, with his falcon on his left hand, accompanied by his hunting dog and surrounded by a fox, a duck, and a dragon-snake, probably the hunter's prey. In the narrow border a variety of real and mythical animals are placed running towards the symbol of a double snake-dragon.

49. Bronze mirror with relief decoration from Iraq. Mid 13th century. diam. 9½ in. (24 cm.). Collection of Fürst Öttingen Wallerstein. The decoration of this cast bronze mirror consists of a complex astrological complex, a popular subject in Seljuk metalwork particularly on mirrors. In the centre is a bird with outspread wings, a motif frequently found in the art of the Seljuks and Atabeks of Iraq and Syria. Around the birds are the busts of the seven planet gods. These busts have close links with classical antiquity. The twelve outer medallions show the signs of the zodiac combined with other planetary figures. The dedicatory inscription contains the name of an Urthukid, suggesting that the object belonged to the Urthukid rulers of northern Iraq. If so, it is one of the very few metalwork pieces of the period that can be associated with that particular region.

ment the rug became of decorative interest, and its long-haired fur, originally on the underside of the fabric, was turned upwards, cut and transformed into the pile of the modern rug.

Seljuk rugs are already the end-product of a long tradition. The main fields have simple repeat patterns, based on highly abstracted floral forms, the borders much bolder abstract patterns based on Kufic writing. Their colours vary—red, blue and white, however, dominating. The variety of patterns within the limited number surviving indicates a highly developed art, and the richness of colour and contrast of the striking border designs with the small-scale field patterns show again the fine sense of design that so often characterises Turkish Seljuk art.

Little is known of Seljuk metalwork in Anatolia, but it would appear that the inlay techniques so elaborately used in Iran were not adopted there. Plastic form seems to have been favoured and engraving is the main element of decoration.

Seljuk art in Anatolia continues many of the principal ideas developed by the Seljuk Turks in Iran. The cultural unity of the Seljuk-dominated part of the Muslim world is demonstrated by identical forms of ceramic painting and tile decoration. In architecture, however, highly original forms are developed that differ fundamentally from those of Iran. The closed prayer hall mosque, and the monumental caravansarayi show a new organisation of architectural space into large enclosed units, and a new attitude in designing buildings to be seen from all sides. Orientation towards the interior, characteristic of Iran, is abandoned and counterbalanced by equal attention to the exterior with special emphasis on the design of façades and general surface decoration. The Seljuk Turks excelled in stone-carving, widely used in architectural decoration, and with the development of faience mosaic they made a contribution to eastern Islamic art that can only be compared in importance to the invention of lustre-painting by the Abbasid potters of Baghdad and Samarra.

The Art of the Atabeks and the Ayyubids

With the division of Seljuk Iran after the death of Sultan Sanjar, 1157, between various of the Seljuks, the regions of Iraq and Syria became independent under the rule of their Atabeks (regents). Various cultural centres developed at the court of these Atabek dynasties. Mosul and Aleppo, capitals of the Zangids, and Damascus, seat of Nur al-din Mahmud ibn Zangi's court, became important in the 12th and early 13th centuries. Diyar Bakr, and later Kayfa and Mardin in Eastern Anatolia—seats of the courts of the Urthukids—became centres of a culture that combined elements of Seljuk tradition with a great many original ideas. Art forms of great interest and beauty were evolved and passed on to the Ayyubids who inherited an artistic tradition of the greatest significance for the further development of western Islamic art.

Egypt came under the sway of the Ayyubids in the second half of the 12th century when Salah al-din Ayyub (Saladin) (1169–93) seized power. An envoy sent to Egypt by Nur al-din Mahmud ibn Zangi (1146–73), Atabek of Syria, Salah al-din changed the kutba (Friday prayer) in Egypt in 1171 having the Abbasid caliph of Baghdad mentioned in it instead of the last, dying Fatimid caliph. With his death in the same year, the Shiah caliphate of Egypt came to an end.

Salah al-din added the Hijaz and the Yemen to his realm, took Tripoli from the Normans and in 1174 annexed Damascus after the death of Nur al-din Mahmud ibn Zangi. It took about ten years to subdue the rest of the country (Aleppo fell to Salah al-din only in 1183) and Iraq. In 1187 Jerusalem was taken from the Christians. The Ayyubid empire was consolidated. The Third Crusade failed to restore Jerusalem to the Christians. On the death of Salah al-din in 1193 the empire was divided between other Ayyubids with Cairo, Damascus and Aleppo as centres. But in 1250 Ayyubid rule came to an end in Egypt with the take-over by their vassals, the Bahri Mamluks, and Iraq and Syria were soon invaded by the Mongols.

ARCHITECTURE

Although little architecture built during Atabek rule survives unaltered or intact, surviving monuments indicate a combination of elements from Seljuk Iran and Anatolia with elements of local pre-Seljuk tradition, especially in Iraq, that provided the basis for the great flowering of architecture in the Ayyubid period.

The Great Mosque in Aleppo, begun in the Zangi period but completed only in 1190 after the take-over by Salah al-

50. **The Congregational Mosque in Aleppo, Syria.**
12th–13th centuries. Probably going back to a very early foundation, this mosque dates mainly from the 13th century. Its minaret, one of the most beautiful in Syria, is also the earliest

monument of the Seljuk period in that country (1090). The marble pavement and the large fountain in the centre of the court, are very fine.

din, bridges both periods and shows a continued artistic tradition from the Atabek to the Ayyubid period in Syria. Its large prayer hall with a beautiful polychrome mihrab, its tall, square stone minaret, and its splendid marble pavement in the large court, are typical of a new simplicity in decorative architecture, with cubic outlines and large undecorated wall surfaces contrasting with delicate but powerfully carved or subtly coloured marble-inlay ornaments.

50

The most impressive monument of pre-Ayyubid architecture is the citadel of Aleppo although most of what survives dates only from the reign of the first Ayyubid sultan of Aleppo, Zahir Ghyath al-din Ghazi (1186–1216). Built at the top of a hill in the centre of the city, the citadel is one of the most formidable fortifications of the Muslim world. Its elaborate entrance structure is most striking with two gate towers connected by a long bridge supported on high, pointed arches of great beauty. This enormous, cubic block has in its lower storey a complicated passage-way with a succession of doors and security devices, leading to a ramp and staircase up to the second storey, which consists almost entirely of a 15th-century reception hall. Partly altered in the Ayyubid and Mamluk periods, the unity of the citadel demonstrates clearly the strength of architectural traditions of this period which were to continue until the 16th century.

25

26

Important buildings were erected all through the 12th and 13th centuries both in Iraq and Syria during Atabek rule; among them the great madrasahs of Baghdad, Aleppo and Damascus are of special significance. The design of the madrasah, developed first in Seljuk Iran and adopted in Seljuk Anatolia, was brought to perfection in the Atabek and Ayyubid periods. Two-storey rooms for students and teachers were arranged around an open court with tall ivan-halls set into the centre of each side. Sometimes a single ivan plan is used, possibly following Anatolian

models. The Ayyubids introduced the design into Egypt where it found monumental expression in Sultan Kalaun's and Sultan Hasan's buildings in Cairo.

Of Ayyubid secular architecture in Egypt Salah al-din's citadel in Cairo is undoubtedly the main example. With Fatimid-style walls, heavily fortified towers and gates, it rivals in many ways the citadel of Aleppo. Though not as elaborate—the Aleppo citadel has more substructures— and perhaps less formidable in its fortification, the Cairo citadel is among the most remarkable examples of military architecture in the Muslim world.

51

Of many mausoleums, that of Imam al-Shafi'i (1211) is probably the finest. Although altered in the interior decoration during later Mamluk restorations by Sultan Kayt Bey, it still exemplifies the standard plan developed during the period, followed for almost three centuries without major changes. This consisted of a large square chamber surmounted by a tall often fluted dome built of brick or stone and usually resting on an intermediary zone of mukkarnas which became increasingly ornate. The mausoleum always contained a mihrab niche, sometimes triple niches or three individual mihrabs set into a richly ornate kibla wall. The plaster decoration of interiors is quite elaborate, entire wall surfaces often covered with abstract and floral patterns. A dominant design feature are blind niches with magnificently powerful conch shells, as in the Cairo mausoleum of the Abbasid Caliphs (before 1242). Exterior decoration is relatively simple—torus moulding running round the lower storey of al-Shafi'i's mausoleum, with a band of simple geometric ornament along the top, the upper storey pierced by double windows, blind niches with the stylised conche shells, with a band of openwork abstract interlaced ornament and triangular serrations along the top.

52

This type of Egyptian mausoleum continued into the Mamluk period.

51. The Citadel of Cairo. Late 12th and 13th centuries, with some later additions. View of the south façade of the northern enclosure seen from the east. The Citadel of Cairo is one of the most formidable military installations of Muslim architecture. Its foundations, most of the present walls and some of its gates and towers go back to Saladin's time (1169–1193), although he did not complete the building himself, leaving Egypt in 1182. His brother and successor al-Adil carried out much of the final work. The most impressive part of the Citadel are its monumental defence towers and complex gate structures which are rivalled only by those of the Citadel at Aleppo. (See plates 25, 26).

PAINTING

During the 12th century a school of painting emerged in Northern Iraq possibly centred in Mosul. Its style is similar to that of the Seljuks although it also developed an iconography of its own (probably absorbing classical traditions of scientific text illustration) with a keener sense of realism. The frontispiece of the Paris *Kitab al-Diryak* of 1199 is a perfect example of the complete adaptation of Seljuk royal and symbolical iconography. So is the frontispiece of another copy of the same text in Vienna undated but probably early 13th-century, which shows Mosul realism in such details as horsemen and the preparation of a meal for the ruler.

Some 13th-century Syrian manuscripts are very close to classical tradition. The finest of the group, an illustrated copy of Hariri's *Makamat*, 1222, shows the absorption of a local Syro-hellenistic tradition into a brilliant new style of expression and movement, completely different in form and spirit from Seljuk painting.

In the school of Baghdad, only known from 13th-century works, both styles meet and to a degree merge, even though the eastern element always seems to dominate slightly. The paintings executed in a copy of the Makamat, 1237, now in Paris, by a painter whose name is recorded in the manuscript, Yahyah ibn Mahmud al-Wasiti, and in another copy in Leningrad, form the main product of the Baghdad school. In their animation and close observation of the details of everyday life these paintings surpass even the more realistic Mosul paintings or those of the 'hellenistic' Fatimid style.

Very little is known about mid-13th-century painting in Iraq and Syria but a double-page frontispiece in a Baghdad manuscript dated 1287, now in Istanbul, proves that the school of painting survived until the very end of the 13th century, in spite of the newly emerging Il-Khanid style of the Mongols in Northern Iran.

This double-page painting demonstrates for the last time the special quality of the Baghdad school, in its realistic rendering of details such as the brick substructure of the building in which the philosophers appear with their scribes and attendants, or in the extraordinary expressiveness of facial features. But the colours have already acquired an abstract quality, with much gold and white and it is obvious that nothing was to follow from this last phase of the school. Soon painting in Iran took an entirely different direction and the strange mixed style that found its apogee in Baghdad survived only in the provincial Mamluk schools.

POTTERY

Little is known about pottery in the region during the Atabeks' rule. It seems to have been made in large quantities in Syria but of 12th- and 13th-century Iraqi wares nothing survives but a group of unglazed relief wares, mostly large vessels. Their main decoration is applied relief concentrated around the tall necks of the often monumental

52. Interior of the Mausoleum of the Imam Shafi'i, Cairo. The interior of this building, erected in the 13th century was decorated in the 15th by Sultan Kayt Bey who placed a new, wooden dome over the square chamber. The design of the resulting intermediary zone and its elaborate decoration are typical examples of the late Mamluk decorative style in architecture.

53. Painting from a manuscript of the Rasa'il ikhawan al-safa *(Epistles of the Sincere Brethren)*, from Bagdad, Iraq. Dated AH 686 (1287 AD). *Authors and Attendants*. Library of the Suleymaniyeh Mosque, Istanbul. $7\frac{7}{8} \times 6\frac{7}{8}$ in. (20 × 17·4 cm.). This is one of the last paintings of the Baghdad school and shows how main characteristics survived to the end: realistic detail a concern with real life, and an exquisite sense of colour and design. It also shows how this style remained almost entirely free of both Seljuk and Mongol influence which had spread from the East to the rest of the Muslim world. Three of the six authors of the text are shown in this half of the double-page frontispiece.

54. The 'Baptistère de Saint Louis' from Syria.
Metal basin with silver inlay decoration. 1290–1310. Made by Muhammad ibn al-Zayn. diam. 19⅞ in. (50·4 cm.), h. 9⅝ in. (24·4 cm.). Louvre, Paris. This superb piece of Mamluk silver inlaid metalwork is in the highly accomplished figurative style developed by the Ayyubids (following the Seljuk tradition.) It is one of the greatest masterpieces of its kind in Islamic art. The master, known only from one other signed piece, but probably the 'author' or at least two other pieces of a very similar kind, was one of the finest artists working in the field of metalwork. In its richness of figurative invention, fine detail, and perfect design, the basin has few equals. Decorated with a central frieze of figures and two narrow corresponding friezes of animals, it is also decorated along the inside rim with elaborate hunting scenes.

vases, mostly of the figurative iconography of Mosul painting but ultimately in the Seljuk tradition. Seated rulers in frontal position with drinking cup in hand, surrounded by courtiers, are set against a background of floral and abstract motifs often in complicated openwork of great beauty and technical skill. The most striking though unexplained feature is a large female mask that frequently appears on these ornaments. It may reflect ancient pre-Islamic traditions recalling masks in the architectural decoration of Hatra. Other pre-Islamic motifs suggest a long tradition of relief ceramic of which little or nothing is known. Unglazed relief decorated pottery has been found in most parts of the Muslim world some of it dating back to the 8th and 9th centuries. This group, however, is unrivalled in quality and interest.

30 The most important 13th-century pottery centre is Syria with Rakka possibly the main source. Of many different types, three are particularly important: one painted with deep brown lustre similar in effect to that used in Seljuk Rayy; a second painted in polychrome underglaze with both floral-abstract and figurative patterns; and a third with mainly floral patterns painted in black under a brilliant green and blue glaze. While the first two types are almost immediately derived from Seljuk pottery and may well have been inspired by the potters that escaped from Rayy at the advance of the Mongols, the last type is an outstanding and original invention by the 13th-century Syrian potters.

METALWORK

In Mosul an early 13th-century school of metalwork undoubtedly owes much to artists from Seljuk Iran but quickly develops an individual style. Some of its engraved and silver inlaid brasses count among the most beautiful and accomplished of the Muslim world. To differentiate between objects made in Mosul and Damascus is exceedingly difficult, especially as no complete study has ever been made of the large number of dated and inscribed pieces. A group of inlaid brasses, all from the first quarter of the 13th century, can be associated with Mosul through artists' signatures, also another group through the appearance of Badr al-din Lulu's (1233–59) name on some of them. The Ayyubids continued the tradition of richly inlaid and largely figurative designs on metalwork and probably produced the finest work of this type. The figurative style, 24 small-scale on most Seljuk and Atabek objects, increases in

size, and often a vessel, usually itself of large size, is decorated with large figures filling most of the surface area. Even the interiors of large basins are now elaborately decorated. The development of facial features, instead of the stereotype of Seljuk and still of Atabek times, is one of the main achievements of Ayyubid metalwork. The figures on Sultan Ayyub's basin or on the *Baptistère de Saint Louis* 54 are full of an extraordinary vitality and realism seldom found in the earlier metalwork.

ENAMELLED GLASS

Figurative decoration in enamel on glass was also developed in Syria in the later 12th and 13th centuries. In earlier pieces a great deal of gold was used especially for background decoration with foreground designs in red, blue, and white enamel, but equally often red was used alone as the colour to 'draw' both abstract and floral designs, and then both background and motifs were painted gold. Some pieces, probably mid-13th-century, literally transplant scenes from manuscript paintings or silver inlaid metalwork onto glass. This long continuation of Seljuk pictorial tradition is perhaps one of the most interesting and important aspects of the art of this period.

In the art of the Atabeks and the Ayyubids Seljuk tradition is brought almost unchanged to Iraq and Syria. It is particularly predominant in the painting of the Mosul school. Later on western tradition, both contemporary or earlier Byzantine, also became important and this dualism characterises much of the art of 12th- and 13th-century Iraq and Syria.

In both countries Seljuk architectural forms are developed and particularly in Syria monumental stone architecture is of great beauty in its simple, cubic forms and precise and highly abstract carved decoration, particularly in contrast with large, smooth, undecorated surfaces. This element of contrast continued in Syria and Egypt for many centuries with the use of polychrome stone inlay on plain walls that may have been derived from Seljuk Anatolia and that is handed down by the Ayyubids to generations of architects both in Syria and Egypt.

The art of 12th- and 13th-century Iraq and Syria forms 41 a bridge between East and West, combining elements of both, and paving the way for the development of the Mamluk style.

42

The Mongol Period

Early in the 13th century the conquest of the Muslim East by the Mongols under Chingiz Khan began. They reached the Seljuk capital of Rayy in 1220, destroyed Baghdad completely in 1258, slaughtering the last of the caliphs. A period of great disturbance and unrest was initiated in the Eastern Islamic world. Although Muslim culture was disrupted for a time (the Mongols adopted Islam only towards the end of the 13th century) western Asia as a whole was to be enriched by the first direct contact with the art and culture of the Far East. This contact was of decisive importance for the development of later Islamic art both in the East and the West.

Although several Persian cities were destroyed beyond repair—among them the capital, Rayy—the country recovered remarkably well from the devastations of the first Mongol assault, but it took the better part of the 13th century before the new Mongol-Islamic art established itself.

ARCHITECTURE

The Mongols made Tabriz their capital and the ruler Ghazan Khan (1295–1304) and his grand vizir, Rashid al-din, constructed entire new quarters with thousands of houses, baths, many mosques and entire university districts with libraries and research institutes. Ghazan Khan's city also contained his monumental mausoleum. Nothing of all this has survived and only a single major monument of the Mongol period, the mosque of Ali Shah, Rashid al-din's rival and successor, is still partly standing. Öljetü (1304–17), Ghazan Khan's successor, had a new capital built, Sultaniya, on a site southwest of Tabriz. Sultaniya was another elaborately planned and richly endowed city, which has also vanished save for the mausoleum of Öljetü, erected between 1307 and 1317. Although ruined, and in danger of collapsing completely, this magnificent domed structure is still one of the finest pieces of Mongol architecture.

Basically Il-Khanid architecture continues the Seljuk tradition. The mosque plan of the Seljuk period was adopted and continued without vital changes except for a gradual elongation of proportions tending towards a general vertical organisation of all decorative elements. Gateway structures were elaborated and the use of blind niche designs for the decoration of interior and exterior walls was perfected. At the same time intricate stalactite structures were employed for purely decorative purposes. Architectural decoration is mainly of plasterwork often applied to the whole building.

The particular plan of a centralised domed or vaulted building without secondary structures and without a court and ivan-hall part, which had been developed and used in Seljuk times, was also adopted by the Mongols. Ali Shah's great mosque in Tabriz, built between 1310 and 1320, is one of the most impressive buildings of the period. Although following Seljuk tradition structural features were often improved upon, especially in their decorative effect. A new widespread feature was a double-shell dome —as in Öljetü's mausoleum—allowing the elevation of an outer dome to a considerable height while covering the inner room with a shallow dome.

Other important forms of Mongol architecture are the tomb tower and Imamzadeh building (or saint's mausoleum), both following pre-Mongol patterns, but again invested with new decorative values. The use of the narrow, elongated blind niche, usually set into rectangular frames, both on the inside and the outside of these buildings, gives them, in addition to their generally slender proportions, a special elegance and appeal.

The mausoleum of Öljetü, originally part of a building complex, stands today as sole survivor of the vanished city. It consists of a monumental dome chamber with a small mortuary chapel on the south side. The gallery encircling the dome supports a platform that originally carried eight minarets. The interior chamber is octagonal in shape—enlarged with deep bays in the centre of each side. The entire building is decorated with a dado of blue glazed tiles in geometrical interlace band designs, with carved and moulded terracotta panels at intervals and painted plaster above the dado. (The original decoration was changed after a plan was abandoned to make the building into a mausoleum for Imam Husayn; all the tile decoration was plastered over and painted with abstract designs in black, blue and brownish-red on a white ground.)

In great contrast is the austere bareness of the immense vaulted ivan-hall of Ali Shah's mosque in Tabriz. Only the inside of the building is relieved to some extent by the upward movement of narrow blind niches counteracting the enormously heavy effect of massive brick walls.

PLASTERWORK

Even though Mongol architecture excelled in the variety of its buildings and in refining the traditional forms, its highest accomplishment lies in the unparalleled richness of its plasterwork in an astonishing variety of techniques. Plaster decoration covered entire wall surfaces and also emphasised certain structural features. The characteristically superb ornament in the interior of Pir-i Bakran—a small mausoleum near Isfahan—ranges from the simple incised line to deeply undercut high relief, from calm abstract linear patterns to almost baroque movements in the large floral and semi-floral abstract patterns. The typically rich and elaborate, carved and modelled mihrab also illustrates the frequent use of calligraphic designs. On one of its three frames of ornament, a beautifully designed double inscription in naskhi and angular Kufic is set against layers of floral scroll and arabesque patterns. Sometimes on walls, infinite linear patterns were created with calligraphic characters running diagonally, repeating again and again the same words—Allah, Muhammad or Ali.

PAINTING

Mongol paintings are the first to survive in large quantities and it is usually with these that histories of painting in the

55. **Masjid-i Jami of Taj al-din Ali Shah, Tabriz, Iran,** c. 1310–1320. The building is exceptional in many ways. It uses a mosque design rare in Iran, that of an open ivan hall without a dome chamber. In size it is matched only by the Mausoleum of Öljetü. Almost undecorated, the effect of the vast brick surfaces is nevertheless most impressive. Only minor adjacent buildings, such as a low open arcade running around a central pool in front of the ivan hall, are later additions.

Muslim East begin. Very largely, however, they follow earlier traditions, Seljuk influence being clearly visible, especially in local styles. The first examples demonstrate particularly well the complexity of pictorial traditions in Mongol Iran.

The earliest evidence of the composite transitional style is in the paintings of the *Manafi al-Hayawan* manuscript (1297, Marageh, near Tabriz). At least three major styles are evident, the traditional Baghdad style, the Seljuk style, and the new, progressive Il-Khanid style, greatly influenced by Chinese painting.

While the Baghdad style miniatures continue to cling to a certain decorative realism, especially in animals and figures, the Seljuk style paintings, of which a few very important ones survive, adopted some features of the Chinese form of landscape while still following their own Central Asian figural tradition as in the magnificent Adam and Eve painting.

Most paintings, however, are already in the new style. Painted with a full brush, in almost impressionistic manner, some of the miniatures come quite close to their Chinese models. A figure of the phoenix, set into a fantastic frame of elaborate foliage, is a brilliant expression of the new style.

Mannered, animated and full of unexpected movement, painted with a brilliant disregard for established traditions and with a zeal for depicting the world and its creatures in a new way, these paintings have an extraordinary freshness and intensity, altogether highly original. Chinese painting did not serve so much as immediate model to be slavishly followed but rather as a catalyst that set free unexpected forces in the artists of the period.

Rashid al-din's *History of the World*, survives in several early 14th-century illustrated copies that show the gradual evolution of an independent Mongol style—although elements of pre-Mongol, Chinese and even western European painting are fused in a strange and not always successful fashion. These illustrations resemble coloured drawings more than actual paintings, being basically linear in design, and often using thin and translucent colours of soft hues.

Very different are the paintings of the main work of the period, the illustrations for a monumental *Shah-nameh*, probably mid-14th-century but possibly later. With strong solid colours, and a fantastic realism unlike anything in Mongol painting in Tabriz, they would appear to have been done by painters of quite another artistic centre,

35

36

56. **Mausoleum of Sultan Muhammad Öljetü Khudabanda.** Sultaniya. 1307–1313. This building, originally part of a complex of structures in the city of Sultaniya, the new capital of the Mongols since 1305, has rightly been claimed to be the finest known example of Mongol architecture, one of the most competent and typical products of Persian Islamic building. It stands in the line of tradition of domed tomb chambers that had been built in the Muslim East since the 10th century. The ingenious distribution of the enormous thrust of the huge dome on a small number of points, making the piercing of the massive walls by niches and windows and gates possible, creates an effect of extraordinary lightness and grace. It served as model for similar mausoleum structures in both Iran and India.

probably fairly distant from Tabriz. The manuscript was split up and only a small number of the original paintings survive. Having fully absorbed the traditions of pre-Mongol Iran and eliminated elements that would not fit into the new imagery, the painters of this extraordinary series of *Shah-nameh* illustrations created an atmosphere of intense emotion and fierce action that is without parallel in Muslim painting. The human figure acquires an individual quality—facial types are abandoned for truly individual features—comparable only to the roughly contemporary Italian Renaissance painting. The combination of the realistic detail of human figures, animals and landscapes with a fantastic iconography, inherited from the tradition of the *Shah-nameh*, creates a unique pictorial
37 style. Powerful in design, strong in colour and exceedingly rich in detail—down to embroideries on a king's coat, a small flower, pebbles on the road or the peculiar twist of a shrub or branch of a tree—these *Shah-nameh* paintings are the highest achievement of eastern Islamic painting. Nothing created at the time, certainly none of the illustrations for some small *Shah-nameh* manuscripts, probably made in or near Tabriz in the 1340s, comes anywhere near them for quality and intensity.

38 The altogether different paintings of the Inju school of Shiraz are mainly drawings, of a sketchy, almost careless nature, often stereotyped in facial expressions or landscape detail. Their main value lies in a highly developed decorative sense, both in design and colour.

Towards the end of the 14th century, on the basis of the pictorial tradition established by the great *Shah-nameh* and the local schools in Tabriz, Baghdad and Shiraz, the governor dynasties of the Jalairids and Muzzaffarids developed a form of painting that emphasised the new spatial concept of Mongol painting. A primitive form of perspective was created by using the larger part of the pictorial area for a landscape setting where groups of men and fighting armies could be displayed on different levels one above the other. This new technique freed the painter from the traditional rigid one-level concept. In the old system all the figures were firmly fixed to a bottom line and extended almost the full height of the picture making any suggestion of space impossible. The new method was of fundamental importance for the further development of painting in the Timurid period.

DECORATIVE ARTS

In the decorative arts the Mongols again followed earlier models to a great extent. In pottery especially they seem not to have been very inventive. Apart from the adoption of a few Chinese types of pottery—such as celadon ware which was probably first imitated in Il-Khanid Iran—the traditional forms of pottery, especially the Kashan lustre-wares, were continued.

Kashan seems only slightly affected by the Mongol conquest and the kilns continued almost without interruption to produce their wares. In the later 13th and early

14th century, the city supplied the country more than ever before with tilework. The famous set of tiles found in Damghan and Veramin, made in the 1260s, and a number of monumental mihrabs follow those of the early 13th century in almost every detail. The only important change is a general tendency towards a heavier lustre coating, a less delicate background pattern and an overall use of additional cobalt blue and turquoise glazes. Kashan lustre-painted pottery continued throughout the first half of the 14th century with only minor changes in style—a certain simplification of designs and background patterns just as in the tiles, and the adoption of a number of typically Chinese motifs.

Towards mid-century, a new form of pottery developed in Iran, usually called Sultanabad ware, as the first examples were found there. Sultanabad ware is, however, probably nothing more than the last stage of the Kashan workshops. There are two distinct types: one is decorated in blue, green and black under a clear glaze on a buff white slip with predominantly floral motifs. Plant or leaf motifs decorate the rims of the little shallow dishes, or the steep-sided bowls with heavy lips. In the centre of the bowl an **40** animal motif or, in rare cases, human figures appear. There is a second variety which has the same shapes but different colours—white and shades of brown and grey. The pottery is almost in all cases heavy, the glaze thick, the designs rather rough in detail.

Of the other decorative arts of the Mongol period metal-**58** work in particular should be mentioned as it again continues Seljuk tradition, but also makes use of the new repertoire of Far Eastern motifs. The elongated, Mongoloid figures, known from early 14th-century paintings in the Rashid al-din's *Jami al-tawarikh* and from Sultanabad pottery, also appear here.

42 The art of the Mongol period in Iran is characterised by a predominantly Far Eastern flavour, although the Seljuk tradition was continued almost without change in architecture and architectural decoration. Glazed tilework and faience mosaic, first employed in the Seljuk period, and especially a magnificent development of plaster decoration transformed the relatively simple traditional forms. But it is in painting and in the minor arts that the Chinese element is most prevalent, stimulating a new inventiveness rather than creating an eclectic attitude. The paintings of the late Mongol period number among the finest in the Muslim world, combining realism and attention to detail with inventiveness and fantasy in an entirely original form of pictorial expression. The Mongol period is of lasting importance for both eastern and western Islamic art providing a large repertoire of decorative forms and ideas to the artists of the Timurid and Safavid periods in Iran and to Ayyubid and Mamluk Syria and Egypt.

57. **Plasterwork decoration of the mihrab of Pir-i Bakran,** near Isfahan. Early 14th century. The rich and varied ornament of this mihrab shows the skill and beauty of carved and modelled plasterwork in the Mongol period, also the use of calligraphic design.

58. **Brass bowl with silver inlay design from Iran.** 14th century. diam. 9½ in. (24 cm.), h. 4⅛ in. (10·5 cm.). Staatliche Museen zu Berlin. Very little metalwork of the Mongol period survives. It seems that with the exodus of metalworkers to Iraq and Syria before the conquering Mongols, the art form declined in Iran. This bowl follows a typical shape developed in the later part of the 13th century and its decoration is equally pre-Mongol. The design itself shows, however, subtle changes in iconography especially in the use of Far Eastern decorative motifs and the manneristic elongation of the human figure.

Mamluk Art

The Mamluks (Mamluk actually means 'owned') were the Turkish slaves of the Ayyubid rulers of Egypt. The first Mamluk dynasty, the Bahri, that came to power in 1250 with the fall of the Ayyubids in Syria and Egypt, were descendents of the slaves of Sultan Salih Ayyub (1240–9). They ruled Egypt and after the defeat of the Mongol army at Ain Jalut in 1260 under the leadership of Sultan Baybars al-Bundugtari (1260–77), also Syria for a century and a half, only to be superseded by the second Mamluk dynasty, the Burji, descendents of the Circassian slaves of the Bahri Mamluk Sultan Kalaun (1279–90). The Burji Mamluks ruled both Egypt and part of Syria until the conquest of the Ottoman Turks at the beginning of the 16th century.

The art of the Mamluk period is closely related to the arts and culture of the Ayyubid period. In fact, there is only a very slow and gradual change in the artistic tradition of Western Islam in the (Seljuk) Atabek, Ayyubid and Mamluk periods.

Mamluk architecture continues almost completely the traditions of Iraq and Syria on the one hand, and of North Africa and Egypt on the other. Thus it combines elements of both the Fatimid and the Seljuk and Ayyubid traditions in evolving a new style of its own. Secular architecture as in the Cairo citadel, largely follows Fatimid models, while the great madrasahs are inspired by Syrian and Iraqi buildings, and the structure of the mosques, such as those of

59. **Interior of the main ivan of the madrasah-mausoleum of Sultan Hasan,** Cairo. 1356–1363. The interior of the main ivan of the madrasah which served as a mosque is typical of decorative design in Mamluk architecture during the second half of the 14th century. There is a striking contrast between blank, undecorated wall space and decorative motifs such as the beautiful relief inscription which runs all around the square room. The mihrab is of particularly rich design with its double recess and double sets of columns. The stone minbar is of equally accomplished quality, particularly the door frame which repeats on a smaller scale the monumental entrance gate to the building.

Sultan Baybars or Kalaun, follow the local tradition, established with the mosque of Ibn Tulun. The building material is mainly stone although brick is also used especially for vaults, arches and domes.

The architecture of this period both in Syria and Egypt is generally of monumental scale. It has great simplicity of form and a distinctly sombre quality. Large, flat, undecorated surfaces are contrasted with deep carving both in form of epigraphic or linear abstract ornament and in form of deep niches often decorated with floral patterns and arabesque work. The upper part of such niches—around dome drums, on mosque façades, above gateways—is often decorated with the traditional serrated conch-shell motif, already encountered as an important element in Fatimid architectural decoration and taken over by the Ayyubids in Egypt. The Ayyubids also passed on smooth-surfaced, precisely cut mukkarnas patterns in gateway or portal designs, which they must have brought into Egypt from 12th-century Syria where these first appeared. Polychrome wall decoration, using coloured stones and marbles, probably also came from Syria. At first used sparingly round gateways, window frames and in mihrab niches, the technique was then applied to large wall surfaces (still in the 13th century) and became the main feature of the decoration of exteriors. The best example of it is Kayt Bey's

madrasah-mausoleum of the second half of the 15th century.

Building activity reaches a new height in Egypt during the reign of Sultan Baybars al-Bundugtari (1260–77). Of his great mosque, built 1266–9, only the walls of the outer enclosure are still standing but most of the original design of the building can be reconstructed. The immense rectangular mosque follows very much the design of al-Hakim's mosque of more than two centuries before (see Fatimids chapter) which, in turn, followed closely the design of Ibn Tulun's, demonstrating how strong the tradition of mosque design derived from Abbasid Iraq had been in Egypt. One feature—a monumental dome chamber in front of the mihrab with a triple aisle transept leading to it—is unique in Egypt at the time and may well have been an import from Iran, from where many artists had fled before the invading Mongols. Dome chamber tracts of a similar nature appear also, however, in some Seljuk mosques in Anatolia from where they may have been transmitted through Syria to Egypt.

Of the madrasah buildings that were erected both in Syria and Egypt during this period and that were probably brought to Egypt by Salah al-din from Syria, the monumental complex of Sultan Kalaun (1279–90) built together with the sultan's mausoleum during the short span of a year in 1284–5, is undoubtedly the most impressive. It

60. **Façade of the Madrasah and Mausoleum of Sultan Kalaun, Cairo.** 1284–5. This impressive complex unites two buildings behind one façade. Its simplicity is typical of early Mamluk style; the cubic quality of the main minaret contrasts strongly with the later slender and elegant minarets.

61. **Interior of the Mausoleum of Sultan Kalaun, Cairo.** 1284. Various materials, including carved and painted plaster, are used to achieve the exquisite richness of surface decoration. The screen on the right separates the central octagonal domed tomb enclosure.

62. The Madrasah-Mausoleum of Sultan Hasan, Cairo.

Built between 1356–63. This is the most important of the
four-ivan madrasahs of the Mamluk period in Cairo. At the end
of the main ivan the square dome chamber of the mausoleum is
placed. The dome is a modern restoration.

combines all the characteristic features of Mamluk
architecture at its best—its cubic monumentality, its
simplicity of form, the restraint and effectiveness of its
exterior surface decoration and its great beauty and richness of interior decoration employing a great variety of
techniques, including plasterwork.

The façade of the building, combines the fronts of both
the madrasah and the mausoleum, which is set back
slightly. A portal between them leads into a long corridor
from which one can turn off into the court of either building. The spacious central court of the madrasah with its
four ivan-halls—two large and two very small and shallow
ones—has its main ivan-hall, a prayer room, at the south
side arranged in a triple aisle basilical form with a façade
in two storeys that repeats the triple arcade motif. Its
particular design recalls earlier solutions of a similar form
in Islamic palace architecture. It also has a certain similarity to the arrangement of a kibla transept in Sultan Baybars'
mosque.

The most interesting feature of these two buildings is
their decoration. Especially noteworthy is the rich application of carved plaster with both epigraphic and floral
motifs. Particularly beautiful is the decoration of the
entrance façade of the mausoleum, pierced by windows
filled with linear grille work in plaster and framed by a
succession of borders with outstanding arabesque work in
clear, precisely cut outlines.

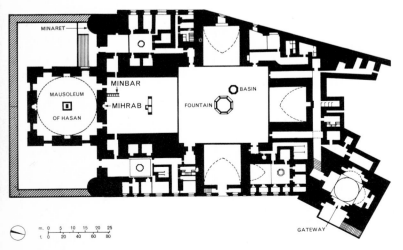

G. Plan of Sultan Hasan's Madrasah-Mausoleum, Cairo.

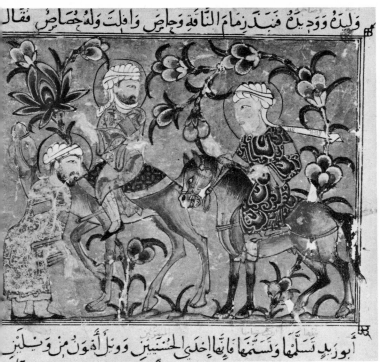

63. Painting from a copy of al-Hariri's Makamat. Egypt. 1337. *Abu Zayid helps al-Harith to regain his stolen camel.* 5¼ × 6¾ in. (13·5 × 17 cm.). Bodleian Library, Oxford. The Bodleian Hariri paintings, although almost certainly creations of the same school that produced the Vienna copy (see plate 43) are much freer in the treatment of both the figures and the decorative floral detail in the landscapes. There is also a more immediate contact with Il-Khanid tradition, especially noticeable in the decorative detail. The painting is full of movement and free of the 'frozen' quality of the Vienna paintings.

64. Ceramic bowl from Cairo. First half 14th century. Inscribed with the name of an officer of Sultan Malik Nasir Muhammad (d. 1341). diam. 10¼ in. (26 cm.) h. 7⅛ in. (18 cm.). A typical Mamluk ceramic vessel, heavy in body and shape and decorated both inside and out with incised inscriptions and monochrome glazes. Very few pieces of Mamluk ceramic ware have survived intact which gives this bowl particular value.

Of 14th-century monuments, the massive complex of the madrasah of Sultan Hasan (built 1354–62) is undoubtedly the most important. Its cruciform shape is made up of four deep ivan-halls with secondary rooms in between, the main ivan leading to a huge dome chamber. The façade is decorated with a series of narrow recessed niches running almost to the full height, giving a vertical direction and rhythm to the heavy cubic block. Its portal is dominated by a colossal central niche filled with elaborate mukkarnas design above and pierced by the entrance gate below. Elsewhere the portal is faced with simple recessed panels and squares of geometric ornament, or small deep niches cut into the lower part of the sides of the entrance hall. The sheer size of the portal structure and the austere simplicity of its decoration make it one of the most powerful pieces of Islamic architecture in Egypt.

During Sultan Kayt Bey's reign (1468–96), a great number of especially magnificent buildings were erected while some buildings of earlier periods were restored and redecorated, including the mausoleum of Imam Shafi'i (see Ayyubid period) which owes its particularly rich surface treatment in the interior to the Mamluk period. Kayt Bey's madrasah-mausoleum has a complicated design. It includes a tomb dome chamber, a four-ivan madrasah, a group of rooms for students and teachers to live in, a public fountain with a school built above it on a second storey, with an open loggia. The wall decoration is

extremely fine and sophisticated, using different coloured stone to brilliant effect on both the exterior and the interior of the building. It is probably the best and most accomplished example of the style developed in the later 15th century.

PAINTING AND DECORATIVE ARTS

Painting in western Islam was deeply influenced by the Far Eastern experience of Iran and a great many motifs and concepts were transmitted from there to the Mamluk realm merging with the local traditions established in the late 12th and early 13th centuries in Iraq, Syria and Egypt. Out of this mixture of traditions, Mongol and pre-Mongol, a strange and powerful style developed that, even though to a certain degree provincial, and eclectic, can still claim a great deal of originality and individual quality. The main body of Mamluk paintings that have survived follows a tradition that is primarily based on the Baghdad style in a considerably abstracted form. In these paintings we encounter a world altogether removed from real life. The contrast is particularly striking since the majority of the Mamluk paintings that have come down to us illustrate the same Makamat text that formed the basis for the great masterpieces of the Baghdad school. Nothing of the almost impressionistic rendering of everyday life that characterised these paintings has been transferred to the Mamluk school. Here all figures are types and all settings ornamental abstractions, representations of ideas rather than real

65. **Brass tray with silver inlay decoration from Egypt.** End of 13th or early 14th century. The inscription contains the name and titles of Sultan Kalaun (1293–1309). Victoria and Albert Museum, London. Diam. 31 in. (78.8 cm.). The tray, one of the most sumptuous of its kind, is a perfect example of the elaborate metalwork of Mamluk Egypt. An entirely new style, only very loosely connected with the Seljuk tradition of Iran and Syria has been created, and the patterns, now exclusively abstract, have taken on a new vitality quite different from the pictorial traditions of Syrian metalwork in the 13th century. The large, radiating inscriptions have the quality of bursting light and lend an element of movement and energy.

66. **Bronze mirror with silver and gold inlay from Syria.** Made by the Master al-Waziri for a Mamluk governor. Mid-14th-century. diam. *c.* 6½ in. (16.7 cm.). Topkapi Sarayi Museum, Istanbul. The unusually well preserved silver inlay of this mirror gives a particularly good idea of the high quality of design and craftsmanship of Syrian metalworkers in the 14th century. The tradition of the 13th century is carried on without interruption but at the same time a richness of detail and a perfection of figure drawing developed that has few counterparts in the earlier work.

objects or landscapes, a fact that is emphasised by the strict use of a highly polished gold background.

In some of the miniatures the important influence that Il-Khanid art had on all 14th-century Islamic painting can be clearly felt. There are floral scrolls with heavy peony blossoms on cloud band forms that are directly derived from Mongol Iran, and even the figure style is somewhat less rigid and abstract.

Very little Mamluk pottery has survived. Again following pre-Mamluk and non-Egyptian traditions, the greater part of Mamluk pottery is distinctly hybrid. There are **41** monochrome glazed wares with carved or incised decorations, and there are polychrome underglaze painted wares that use mainly black and blue, following in their floral and animal designs Syrian and Persian models.

Mainly produced in Syria, and continuing an earlier tradition, but equally common in Egypt, was a very fine sgraffito ware with bright yellow or a buff white as the main colour and brilliant greens, blues and a brownish red as its palette. The incised designs are largely floral in the background, often with a large figure, human or animal, as the main motif.

The most original and unmistakably Egyptian Mamluk ware is of an entirely different nature. It is heavy, thickly glazed and of a very distinct intense colouring, green, brown, yellow, one colour usually being used for the main

67. Kursi (cupboard for a Koran) from Cairo. Made for
Sultan Kalaun in AH 728 (1327–8 AD). diam. 15⅜ in. (39 cm.)
h. 27½ in. (70 cm.). Museum of Islamic Art, Cairo.
Egypt took the lead in metalwork in the late 13th century
and throughout the 14th and 15th centuries objects were
produced there in great quantity and of the finest
quality. This tall *kursi*, engraved, silver inlaid and perforated
with arabesque designs, is not only complex, but also extremely
accomplished.

part of the glaze with details of the pattern in another. The
decoration consists almost exclusively of inscriptions and
typically Mamluk heraldic emblems, being picked out in a
second and third colour. The effect is sombre and powerful
in the simplicity of design and the intensity of the deep
colours. The shapes, steep walled bowls, round pots and
footed cup-bowls, are fairly heavy and not terribly elegant,
but they add to the effect of solidity and strength, qualities
characteristic of all Mamluk art.

During Mamluk rule Cairo took the lead in the production of metalwork. Inheriting the early 13th-century tradition of inlaid brasses transmitted to Egypt by the Ayyubids,
Mamluk metalwork quickly developed a style of its own.
The rich figure style of the Seljuk tradition, continued and
brought to unsurpassed height by the Ayyubids, was
abandoned and replaced by a purely non-figurative style.
The objects, basins, ewers and trays, candlesticks and
incense burners of circular form, become large in scale and
powerful in design. The areas of silver and gold inlay with
their monumental inscriptions and rich floral design, a
repertoire largely of Mongol or Far Eastern inspiration,
give these objects a truly magnificent appearance. A great
many pieces are inscribed with the name of the sultan for
whom they were made or with the names of officers of the
Mamluk court, making a precise dating of individual
pieces or of groups of objects possible. It seems that the
highest achievement was in the 14th century and there was
a decline in the 15th century. Inlay technique was abandoned and instead a rather coarse and limited engraving
technique was developed. The shapes of the vessels got
clumsier and heavier, in strange contrast to the magnificence of architectural decorations of the 15th century, under
Sultan Kayt Bey. Finally the decoration of metal objects
fell into almost complete decline.

During the long period of Mamluk domination of Syria
and Egypt a style of architecture and architectural decoration was developed that united the various elements
derived from Fatimid, Seljuk, and Ayyubid art. The building material was again largely stone, and the basic forms
are of monumental and highly abstract cubic design. A
contrast was created between austere exteriors and richly
decorated interiors but in the later Mamluk period the
principle of rich decoration in a variety of media—plaster,
relief carving, decorative painting, stone and marble polychrome—was extended to the exteriors as well as the
interiors of buildings.

The decorative arts also followed the principle of simple
and relatively austere forms developing however very
sumptuous effects in the rich silver inlaid brasses of the 14th
century. Painting has only a short period of flowering in the
14th century again reflecting in its abstraction of the Baghdad tradition the non-figurative nature of Mamluk art
which achieved its most succesful forms in the realm of
abstraction.

Nasrid Art in Spain

After the fall of the Umayyad dynasty of Cordoba before the middle of the 11th century, a series of minor dynasties came to power in Spain which ruled the country with various degrees of success throughout the remainder of the century. During the 12th century Spain became largely dependent on or actually part of North Africa under the rule of the Berber dynasties (Almoravides and Almohades). It was only with the Nasrids (1232–1492) that a new cultural impetus was given to the once more unified and politically stable country. At their court in Granada the Nasrids created a culture that reached a level of magnificence unparalleled in Muslim Spain, recapturing the splendour of the first great Islamic period under Umayyad rule. Muslim rule came to an end in Spain in 1492 with the expulsion of the last Nasrid king, Muhammad Buabdil, by Ferdinand and Isabella of Castile.

ARCHITECTURE AND ARCHITECTURAL DECORATION

The most remarkable achievement of Nasrid Spain is the

H. Plan of the Alhambra Palace, Granada

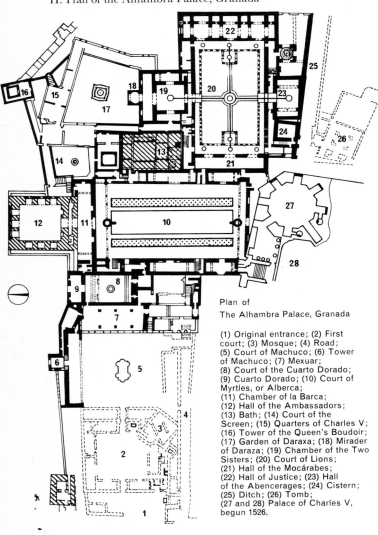

Plan of
The Alhambra Palace, Granada

(1) Original entrance; (2) First court; (3) Mosque; (4) Road; (5) Court of Machuco; (6) Tower of Machuco; (7) Mexuar; (8) Court of the Cuarto Dorado; (9) Cuarto Dorado; (10) Court of Myrtles, or Alberca; (11) Chamber of la Barca; (12) Hall of the Ambassadors; (13) Bath; (14) Court of the Screen; (15) Quarters of Charles V; (16) Tower of the Queen's Boudoir; (17) Garden of Daraxa; (18) Mirador of Daraza; (19) Chamber of the Two Sisters; (20) Court of Lions; (21) Hall of the Mocárabes; (22) Hall of Justice; (23) Hall of the Abencerages; (24) Cistern; (25) Ditch; (26) Tomb; (27 and 28) Palace of Charles V, begun 1526.

building of the Alhambra Palace in Granada. The palace, built at the top of the hill overlooking the city of Granada during the rule of Yusuf I (1333–53) and Muhammad V (1353–91), is of curiously irregular plan, possibly following North African models. It is divided into various separate units each arranged around a central court. The original entrance to the palace was on the west side and the first succession of courts with their adjacent structures runs from west to east. The second part of the palace changes direction, running from north to south. Its main element is a large, oblong rectangular court, the Court of Myrtles, and the Hall of the Ambassadors at the north end. The last part of the palace, arranged around the famous Court of Lions, is again on a west-east axis. It was reserved for the harim and was inaccessible to anyone but the king, his family and their servants. Between these two main palace complexes there was a bath hall, and, in the north-east, a beautiful garden, accessible only from the Court of Lions. The most magnificent of the rooms in the Alhambra, the square Chamber of the Two Sisters, adjoins the private garden its doors opening onto porticos on every side.

In its intricate succession of rooms and courts, constantly changing direction, the richness of surrounding arcades, water basins and water courses, that penetrate into the interior of the building, and with its multitude of fountains, the Alhambra Palace is like a splendid oasis remote from the reality of this world. This effect is especially emphasised through the contrast between an almost entirely undecorated exterior and the unparalleled richness of the interior.

In the Alhambra the fundamental elements of Islamic architecture and basic ideas of architectural design and decoration, developed over many centuries, found their highest form of realisation. In this sense the Alhambra is probably the most perfect piece of Islamic architecture.

Above a tile dado every wall surface is covered with a plaster coating that is decorated with patterns of astonishing intricacy. A great variety of floral, and semi-abstract floral forms (arabesques) are combined with a succession of arch and cartouche motifs, and enriched by highly decorative epigraphic patterns that often merge completely with the abstract linear elements of the patterns, though still remaining readable. There is a strange but highly successful contrast between this intricacy of pattern and the linear and geometric organisation of large units of the walls into panels, bands, cartouches, or frames for doors and windows. The low relief patterns, superimposed in various layers one upon the other, were all gilded and painted in various shades of blue, red and green, transforming the walls into brilliant lacework, an effect heightened by actual openwork in some of the mukkarnas arches of the court arcades. While the material substance of the walls is thus dissolved, the vaulting system, consisting in the main rooms of the most intricate and elaborately designed muk-

(Continued on page 129)

62. Sulaymaniyeh Cami, Mosque of Sultan Sulayman, Istanbul. Founded on July 15th, 1550, and erected by Sinan. Centre of a vast complex of pious foundations, türbes (tombs), hospitals, caravansarayis (rest-houses for caravans), etc., the Suleymaniyeh has since its foundation been the main mosque of the city of Istanbul. Sulayman waited thirty years after becoming Sultan before commissioning the mosque; he obviously had in mind a building of exceptional quality and magnificence and he commissioned the greatest master of his day. This is, moreover, undoubtedly Sinan's finest building. The mosque is placed in the centre of a rectangular enclosure of which the sides are in the proportion of 2:3. The entire organisation of the mosque follows strict proportional relationships (the relationship of the distance between the main gate of the enclosure to the gate of the forecourt, forecourt to mosque, mosque to graveyard behind the mosque is 4:5:5:7). In this respect it is perhaps the most carefully designed of Sinan's building complexes.

81. **Painting from a copy of Firdusi's Shah-nameh,** copied in Tabriz for Shah Tahmasp in 1537. *Rustam defeating the Khakan of Cin.* page: $18\frac{1}{2} \times 12\frac{1}{2}$ in. ($47 \times 31 \cdot 7$ cm.). Collection of Arthur H. Houghton, Jr., New York. The paintings in this manuscript, the most sumptuous of the entire period, executed by the leading masters of the Tabriz school, are perhaps the finest ever produced in Shah Tahmasp's workshop. This painting is outstanding in technique, balance of composition, and subtlety of colour. The dramatic combat between the hero, Rustam, and the Emperor of China in the foreground is counterbalanced by the static effect of the two armies arranged to the right and left of the landscape. A tall tree in the centre gives a final accent of symmetry to the composition.

82. **Painting from a dispersed copy of Firdusi's Shah-nameh,** made in Shiraz. Second half of the 16th century. *The Birth of Rustam.* $11\frac{1}{4} \times 7\frac{1}{4}$ in. ($28 \cdot 6 \times 18 \cdot 4$ cm.). Metropolitan Museum of Art, New York. This is a typical product of the later Shiraz school following a tendency toward abstract pattern and vivid colour already established in the late 15th century. The extreme realism of this subject is unusual in Islamic painting and its choice demonstrates the interest in realistic detail developed by the Shiraz painters in the 16th century.

68. **Stalactite cupola in the Alhambra Palace in the Chamber of the Two Sisters** (room 19 on plan H). 14th century. Granada, Spain. This is undoubtedly the most elaborate use of stalactites (mukkarnas) in architectural design devised by Muslim architects. The complete dissolution of the vault and cupola into a fantastic honeycomb of hanging stalactites, gives the effect of a floating canopy. It demonstrates most eloquently the Islamic preoccupation with the dissolution of matter.

68 karnas domes in the history of Islamic architecture, furthers the immaterial nature of the building.

One of the most profound aspects of Islamic architecture, the illusion of a building floating above the ground, was perfectly realised at the Alhambra. The repetition of motifs, such as the mukkarnas arches in the Hall of Justice, the double, triple, and quadruple finger-thin columns in the main court of the eastern palace, enhance the effect of insubstantiality.

THE DECORATIVE ARTS

This particular quality of Nasrid architecture in 13th- to 15th-century Spain, only equalled in Maghrib architecture, to which the Nasrids are undoubtedly indebted, can also be found in the decorative arts of the same period. Lustre-painting, for instance, with its dematerialising sheen was developed to a new height in Spain, especially in Granada. The technique was probably imported from Egypt, and it is not impossible that lustre ware was actually already made in pre-Nasrid times in Spain, but most of the finds of pottery of this type seem to be imports from Iraq and Egypt. In the 14th and 15th centuries ceramic workshops developed in Malaga, where the tiles that were used in the decoration of the Alhambra and other Nasrid palaces were also made. They are of plain, dull colours, red, brown, green, blue and white, with simple, purely abstract linear decoration. They often have in slight relief the coat of arms of the Nasrids, 'No victory but God's'. The earliest lustre vessels made in Malaga—usually large vases with 'wing'-shaped handles, tall necks, and pointed bases, suggesting that they usually hung in stands—are decorated with various floral (arabesque) and figurative patterns, the latter consisting of confronted animals, in a reddish lustre of beautiful sheen. The decoration is organised in bands,

69. **Ceramic vase with lustre-painted decoration.** 14th century. Malaga (?), Spain. h. 47¼ in. (120 cm.). Alhambra, Granada. Painted in gold lustre with arabesque and animal motifs, using additional cobalt blue to heighten the colour effect, this is one of the earliest of the so-called 'Alhambra Vases', using a form that seems not to have been in use anywhere else in the Muslim world and the most ambitious ever undertaken by Islamic potters. The pear-shaped body, the high, narrow, funnel neck, and the wing-shaped handles on the shoulders of the vase (only one handle is preserved in this piece) are characteristic.

not dissimilar to the geometrical units into which the walls of the Alhambra palace were divided. The most famous piece of this type is the large vase in the Alhambra palace *69* and the entire group are often referred to as 'Alhambra Vases'.

A large number of pieces with coats of arms of the leading families of Europe show the popularity of the ware outside Spain. In Sandwich, Kent, papers have been found recording the export of lustre-painted ware from Malaga in the early 14th century. It seems that interference of the Christian navies with the export of this pottery in the 14th century forced the potters to migrate to the north where they settled near Christian Valencia which then became the main centre of lustre-painted pottery throughout the 15th century.

These vessels are solidly made and the clays are red, porous and not very pure. The glazes are thick, tend to run, and are again impure. But the quality of the lustre, and especially of the lustre-painting is superb and has few rivals in the long and complex history of lustre-painting in the Muslim world. Magnificent grape-vine patterns, abstract linear and heraldic patterns, and occasional large-scale representations of magnificent heraldic beasts, bulls, lions, eagles and falcons, cover the entire surface (often also the outside) of large plates, which are a favoured shape. Cobalt blue is sometimes added which give the plates a most sumptuous and highly decorative air.

Textile weaving, especially of gold brocade but also in tapestry and embroidery, were equally highly developed during this period, and a great variety of other decorative arts testify to the magnificence of this small but remarkably stable and active court.

It is also from this period that the earliest knotted rugs, preceded only by the small group of rugs from Seljuk Anatolia, have survived. They are of great beauty and originality in design, using few and subdued colours, mainly a dull grey, some green, brown, red and blue, a little white and a bit of black for details. Their small-scale repeat patterns, entirely abstract in nature and reminiscent **44** of the complex wall decorations of Nasrid palaces, are of great fascination and have few parallels in other Islamic carpets that we know. Small stars, knots, and other geometric and linear motifs cover the long narrow fields in rhythmic order, while in the narrow borders, usually treated in a somewhat livelier and more colourful manner, a curious and not altogether explained figurative iconography is developed that may have connections with the art of Coptic Egypt.

Nasrid art excels, then, in highly refined decorative effects; a sublimation of architectural decoration that led to a near perfect realisation of that most ardently desired result, the complete dematerialisation of matter; and a variety of decorative arts that number among the most successful in the art of Islam.

The Timurid Period

Mongol culture came to an end and a new era began in eastern Islamic art with the invasion of Iran by Timur (Tamerlane) from Kesh, south of Samarkand. Having consolidated his power among his own people, the Chagatay Turks in Central Asia, Timur descended upon the Islamic world in the second half of the 14th century. He raided Iran and Iraq taking Shiraz, Tabriz and finally Baghdad, and defeated the Ottoman Turks who had just established a new unified empire in Anatolia after a period of unrest after the fall of the Seljuks.

At first Timurid art drew heavily on pre-Timurid tradition and it is not before the consolidation of Timur's conquests by his son, Shah Rukh, who ascended the throne after his father's death in 1405, that Timurid culture came into its own.

ARCHITECTURE

Many features of Timurid architecture, especially in architectural decoration, can already be found during the rule of the Muzzaffarids and Jalairids, local governor dynasties in western and south-western Iran that developed in the later part of the 14th century a culture of great refinement in almost all fields of the visual arts. Particularly close to the later Timurid solutions of architectural design and decoration are the mosques in Kerman of about 1349 and in Yezd, built around 1375, but there is an equally important local (Central Asian) tradition of pre-Timurid art that furnished the Timurids with an abundance of models—especially in architectural design.

The first important monuments of Timurid architecture stand in Central Asia. In Samarkand, Timur's capital, buildings of all phases of Timurid culture have survived although some are now in ruins. Samarkand continued to be a flourishing centre of the arts throughout the 15th century although no longer the capital of the Timurid empire, after the conqueror's death, when Shah Rukh moved his court to Herat.

Shah-i Zindeh, the necropolis outside the city of Samarkand, preserves a variety of small tomb-buildings of simple plan but most exquisite decoration. Built on a square plan with a dome, most buildings have a shallow ivan-hall entrance gate in the centre of an elaborately decorated façade, the whole surface being covered with glazed tilework, usually moulded in relief and glazed in deep cobalt and turquoise blues; carved tilework of metallic abstract arabesque designs, glazed greenish-blue or green; carved and moulded tilework of intricate composite patterns, inscriptions glazed blue and green; and finally plain glazed tiles, green, blue, white and bright yellow.

The domes, often fluted, are decorated with either plain blue and turquoise glazed tiles or bricks or with linear patterns of different coloured tiles. In some tombs even the larger part of the interior is decorated with carved and moulded tilework. But also stucco reliefs and painting were used to complete the richness of the effect. It is from these buildings that one has to reconstruct the lost splen-

(margin references: 46,47 · 48,50)

70. **Ruin of a gate structure of the Ak-Saray, Timur's Palace, Kesh** (Shahr-i Sabz, the Green City). Built between 1390 and 1405. Shahr-i Sabz was the second capital of Timur's empire and it appears that he intended to transfer the capital there permanently from Samarkand. Of the many important buildings erected by Timur only a few remain and those are in ruined state. The palace, of which this monumental gate structure originally formed a part, was observed by Clavijo, the Spaniard who accompanied an embassy to Timur's court in the early 15th century, and it is through his description that we have an idea of its general appearance although it was unfinished when Clavijo saw it. Apart from its size, the most remarkable feature of this architecture is the delicacy of the surface decoration carried out in glazed brick, marble, and faience mosaic.

I. Plan of the Bibi Khanum, Samarkand.

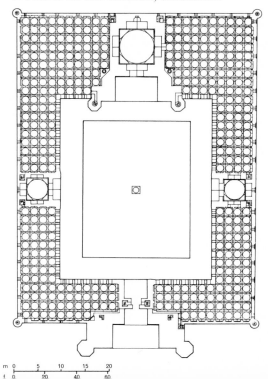

m 0   5   10   15   20
f 0   20   40   60

dours of Timur's, Shah Rukh's and Ulugh Beg's palaces in Samarkand and Herat.

Of Timur's great palace, the Ak-Saray in Shahr-i Sabz (Kesh), built around 1400 and still unfinished when Ruy Gonzalez de Clavijo, Spanish envoy and traveller, saw it in 1403, only the towering ruin of the inner gateway, which led to Timur's audience hall, still stands and shows some magnificent tile-mosaic decoration. According to Clavijo's description, the palace had a succession of enormous gateways with domed reception halls leading into huge court-yards with water basins and fountains and tall buildings on all sides.

Of Timur's Great Mosque in Samarkand, popularly known as the Bibi Khanum mosque, begun in 1399, only ruins remain but they convey once more the monumentality of design and magnificence of decoration in the original building. It has a number of remarkable features. The main portal is unusually large and is on the same axis as the main ivan at the other side of the vast court which has the same design. It has the Seljuk mosque four-ivan plan but with elevated dome chambers behind the two side ivans. These differences in design all add to the imposing character of the mosque which with its rich decoration and enormous proportions must have been one of the greatest achievements of Timurid architecture.

The Gur-i Amir, Timur's tomb in Samarkand, which he intended as a tomb for his nephew but then converted into a family mausoleum, was completed in 1405, the year of his death. Here again traditional architectural concepts are writ large. A huge, fluted, slightly bulbous overhanging dome, rises above a simple polygonal chamber, square on the inside. Its main feature is again a particularly highly developed scheme of coloured faience decoration.

Of the great mosques and palaces that were built by Timur's sons and grandchildren in Samarkand, Herat and in Iran very little survives. Gauhar Shad, Shah Rukh's wife had a family mausoleum built near the city: its beautiful central dome-chamber still stands, testifying to the refinement of architectural design and decoration of the period. The plan, a simple square chamber surmounted by a high fluted dome on a polygonal drum, takes up an earlier concept (also in the idea of a double-dome) that had been inherited from the Mongols, used widely in Shah-i Zindeh and in Timur's mausoleum, and continued to be used in eastern Islamic art in the following centuries. In its particularly fine vaulting system and the beautiful painted interior and faience mosaic exterior decoration the building surpasses all earlier structures.

Little has survived of later Timurid architecture. Incessant warfare between the princes of the realm after Shah Rukh's death in 1447, and the invasions of Uzbeks and Turkomans who gradually took over large parts of the Timurid empire, caused great destruction.

The most important monument of later Timurid architecture was actually not built by a Timurid prince but by the daughter of Jahan-Shah, ruler of the Kara-Kuyunlu Turkomans who had taken over most of western and southern Iran. The Blue Mosque in Tabriz, erected in 1465, has no court and centres around a large dome chamber surrounded by smaller domed rooms. All in all there are eight domes, plus one above a dome chamber that is placed on axis with the main central dome at the rear. The design, although finding certain parallels in Central Asia, is quite original and unusual in Iran. It has been suggested that Byzantine church designs may have served as models, but it seems more likely that contact with Turkish Anatolia is responsible for the plan, as it was in Anatolia that multiple dome structures were first developed in Islamic architecture. The faience decoration of the Blue Mosque is of dazzling beauty and its individual floral and calligraphic designs most delicate.

PAINTING

Little was left of the Mongol school of painting when Shah Rukh ascended to the throne, but he collected what he could still find of Rashid al-din's manuscripts of the *World History* which he ordered to be copied, enlarged and illustrated in his court workshop at Herat. Much of the style of painting of Shah Rukh's court is therefore a somewhat archaicising and slightly modified version of the Mongol style of the early 14th century.

The true Timurid style developed, however, on the basis of a different tradition. After the collapse of Mongol power, the local governor dynasties, the Jalairids and Muzzaffarids, had developed a style of painting in Shiraz and Baghdad, that must be considered one of the sources of inspiration for the new Timurid style at Miran Shah's court in Tabriz, in Shiraz, and a little later in Herat where Baysunghur, Shah Rukh's youngest son, had taken up residence. It is, in fact, the Herat school, under Baysunghur's guidance, that finally develops the classical Timurid court style.

The most important element of the initial new style is the emphasis on a new concept of space. The entire pictorial area was used, showing numerous figures, either singly or in groups, on various planes, through the simple device of introducing a high horizon. This technique of making most of the pictorial area a landscape ground meant that different levels of perspective were represented one above the other on the page. The entire surface of the page could become a flowery meadow or garden in which trees and shrubs would appear in different positions leading up to the high horizon. Mountain ranges were introduced into landscapes behind which further stretches of physical space could be imagined, often suggested by having entire armies emerging from behind the hills. Although the principles of this technique were derived from the pre-Timurid Muzzaffarid and Jalairid painting, space was first conveyed in this way in mid-14th-century Mongol miniatures.

The first phase of the Timurid classical style is encountered in a number of manuscripts that were made for Sultan Iskandar at the beginning of the 15th century. The finest

71. **Painting in a copy of Sadi's Bustan,** painted by Bihzad in 1489, Herat School. Second half 15th century. Page size 11⅞ × 8½ in. (30 × 21·5 cm.). National Library, Cairo. The paintings in this manuscript are generally considered to be the major work of the leading master of the Herat school, Bihzad. This particular painting is signed by the painter and dated. Perfecting and revitalising the style and adding a certain amount of realistic detail, Bihzad's work represents the quintessence of the Herat school of painting which had been developed over a period of almost a century starting with the Baysunghur workshop of the early 15th century (see plates 57, 58).

53, 54 of these is an Anthology made in 1410. In the paintings of this manuscript there are all the qualities that became the standard of excellence in early Timurid painting: the new fully developed spatial concept; a figure style of great elegance and animation; finely observed individual characterisation; the highest technical skill in composing complex groups or postures of individual figures, and a convincing relationship between the individual figures or groups.

The figures are tall and slender. They have oblong heads often with pointed beards, slanting eyes, straight delicate noses and small mouths. They are shown in a great variety of postures, and although their gestures are rather stereotyped, they are extremely animated, always participating fully in the action of a given scene or situation.

The colours are bright without being loud. There is great subtlety of shades and the colours are always used with an eye to the general effect. Much gold is used, and occasionally silver for the representation of water.

53, 54 The paintings in the Sultan Iskandar Anthology rep-

resent what one might call the 'Imperial Timurid style', that is the style that dominated the Timurid realm before the local schools of Shiraz, Tabriz, Herat and the northern provinces developed.

Already around 1420, Shiraz artists were producing paintings of a highly personal nature, closely related to the earlier tradition but different enough to be immediately recognisable. The Shiraz painters of the 1420s and 1430s employed fewer figures and developed a highly mannered landscape. Single figures and small groups of fairly large individual figures are set against mountains and curious rock formations of fantastic shapes and colours. The bodies of the figures are elongated and mannered in pose and gesture; the faces are standardised, expressionless, remote. The colours, pale blues, greys, pinks and whites, dominate landscapes that are almost without vegetation. A few strong local colours are used for animals, human figures, their costumes, and minimal architectural settings.

In about 1420 Herat took the lead. Baysunghur assembled at his court the major talents of his time, producing in quick succession a series of illuminated manuscripts of the highest order. He had various sources to draw upon—the archaistic Mongol-Timurid style of Shah Rukh's workshop, the Imperial Timurid style of ten years earlier, the Shiraz style so well known to him from his residence in his brother's city and from an Anthology made in Shiraz for him on his brother's order, and a local Central Asian tradition that had developed from the immediate contact with Chinese painting.

Of this local tradition, which must have been established at Timur's court in Samarkand and continued there under his grandson Ulugh Beg, and at Shah Rukh's court in Herat, very little is known; a great many paintings have **55, 56** survived in albums in Istanbul that seem to have been painted around 1400 in Samarkand and Herat. We know that various delegations went to and fro between the Timurid and the Chinese court and that Timurid and Chinese painters met and knew each other's works. Copies of Chinese paintings and studies of Chinese motifs in new combinations to be joined into a new pictorial unity, have survived in great numbers.

It is into this line of tradition that the Iskandar **52** Anthology and related illustrated manuscripts of the late 14th and early 15th century fit best. On this basis, Baysunghur's artists formed a new kind of painting. The Baysunghur style perfects the ideals established in the first twenty years of Timurid rule. The refinement of brushwork is unsurpassed, and the sense of subtle colour combinations sublime. There is a further emphasis on well-balanced compositions, a full use of the decorative ideas of landscape design first developed in Shiraz at the end of the 14th and at the beginning of the 15th century and a serenity of mood that can truly be called 'classical'. The Gulestan *Shah-nameh*, made for the bibliophile prince in **57** 1430, contains the most brilliant series of paintings in this style.

The ideals formulated in the Gulestan *Shah-nameh* miniatures became those of all later eastern Islamic painting. The immediate continuation of Baysunghur's style is demonstrated by a number of manuscripts that were produced after the prince's death. Among them the most extraordinary is the copy of the Mir Haydar's *Miraj-nameh* written in eastern Turkish in Herat in 1436. The paintings follow in all major elements the Baysunghur style, but have a more dramatic quality.

The figures are greatly enlarged, very likely a reflection of a tradition of monumental wall-painting carried through from the early Timurid period, of which nothing has survived but which we know of through contemporary reports; and there is an intensity of expression, an emphasis on fantastic-realistic detail, that is so far unique in Islamic painting. It is important to realise that the Turkish (Central Asian) element in Timurid culture was always very strong and it seems that old Central Asian traditions were revived in these paintings.

The disturbed political situation of the mid-century did not favour the art of painting which flourished again only later in the century. The late Herat school is a final flourish of the Baysunghur style. Many elements of the early style that, by the middle of the 15th century had become stereotype formulas, are filled with new vigour and expression. Bihzad, the greatest name in eastern Islamic painting, worked at Sultan Husayn's court and in the paintings of Sadi's *Bustan* in Cairo, of around 1495, the late Herat style achieves its finest form. Bihzad, who lived on into the following century, carried the Timurid style and its ideals into Safavid painting. He surrounded himself with many painters of the greatest skill who collaborated with him in a series of manuscripts made for Sultan Husayn's library. Among these, Mirak-nakkash, Abd al-Razzaq, and Kazim Ali (Qazim Ali) may be mentioned, artists who, between 1480 and 1495, created miniatures for a number of Nizami, Saadi and Mir-Ali Shir Nevai manuscripts that are among the finest products of Muslim art.

In contrast to the Herat tradition which undoubtedly dominated the scene in Central Asia and eastern Iran, the Shiraz school went its own way. The post-imperial style gradually developed into a strange, lifeless stereotype of purely provincial quality—only to be revived and channelled into a new and highly original direction by the Turkoman rulers who took over Shiraz in the middle of the 15th century.

The Turkoman style, in its vigorous colours, lively scenes of action, bold patterns of design, and highly original iconography, belongs to the best and most interesting of the minor schools of Islamic painting. The major work is the series of more than a hundred large and powerful paintings of completely new design which illustrate a text by Ibn Husam, the *Khavaran-nameh*, copied in Shiraz around 1480.

72. **Binding of a copy of Jalal al-din Rumi's Mathnawi,** Herat, AH 887 (1483 AD). Leather. $10\frac{1}{4} \times 7$ in. ($26 \times 17 \cdot 6$ cm.). Museum for Turkish and Islamic Art, Istanbul. The technique used for this bookbinding was first developed in the early 15th century in Herat. The entire pattern is cut out in a kind of filigree technique and pasted upon a coloured leather background. The landscape with various animals—monkeys in trees and flying ducks above—is repeated in the border, thus following the bookbinding traditions of the early 15th century. Such bindings must have been produced in large numbers since albums at the Sarayi in Istanbul contain numerous decorative drawings which must have served as models.

73. **Bronze cauldron with relief decoration.** Inscribed with the name and titles of Timur. AH 801 (1399 AD). diam. $7\frac{1}{2}$ feet (245 cm.). Hermitage, Leningrad. The magnificent cauldron in the form of a large bowl on a high foot (a shape known in Islamic metalwork for several centuries, see also fig. 40) was originally in the Mosque of Ahmad Yassavi in Turkestan. It was obviously a pious donation of the emperor to the mosque which he had erected in 1397.

79. Drawing of a dragon in foliage from Istanbul, Turkey. Mid-16th-century. 6⅞ × 15¾ in. (17·5 × 40 cm.). Museum of Art, Cleveland. Following a tradition going back to at least the early 15th century in Central Asia, this drawing belongs to a school of decorative design that had reached a high level in Herat, and then was transferred at the beginning of the 16th century to Tabriz. From Tabriz it was transmitted to Istanbul in the first half of the 16th century. The drawing was undoubtedly appreciated at the time since it was included in a selection of miniatures, drawings and calligraphy assembled in one album. The famous album in Vienna made for Murad III in 1572 contains a number of such designs.

minute floral rosettes in a pale or blackish blue on a white ground.

68 The blue and white wares give way to pieces of more elaborate, less abstract, and eventually mainly floral designs of a fairly realistic nature. Large lancette and palmette designs and arabesque patterns come into fashion and purple, green and various shades of blue are added to the palette. Important works of this phase are a number of 64 large mosque lamps made for the Dome of the Rock in Jerusalem, which was restored by the Ottomans in the middle of the century and extensively redecorated with tiles on the outside, giving new impetus to the production of tiles, also made for the mosques in Istanbul. Some of these mosque lamps are dated around the mid-century, providing a useful chronology otherwise almost completely lacking in Ottoman pottery.

The final development of Ottoman pottery is a polychrome style of decoration. The motifs are almost exclusively floral, realistic, and particularly sensitive in design. In a few rare pieces animal and bird motifs are included. A brilliant red, applied so thickly as to create a slight relief effect, is one of the most remarkable achievements of the Isnik potters. The secret of this particular colour seems to have been well-guarded as it appeared in no other school of ceramics of the period. Safavid workshops that produced the polychrome 'Kubachi' wares tried persistently to imitate the Ottoman red; they struggled equally unsuccessfully to produce a glaze that would match the purity, brilliance, and durability of the Isnik wares. Isnik pottery, in fact, is unrivalled in the 16th century.

PAINTING AND DRAWING

Little is known of early Ottoman painting and although undoubtedly paintings were produced at the Ottoman court in Bursa before the conquest of Constantinople it is difficult to determine which of the small number of early Turkish paintings date from the pre-Istanbul period. After this conquest and the establishment of a court school under Mehmet's patronage in the palace, Ottoman painting took a distinctive step of its own.

A large group of decorative drawings—mainly of dragons in landscapes or battles between dragons, the phoenix and other real and fantastic animals—and dec-

orative studies of lancette leaf motifs with palmette blossoms of a decidedly calligraphic quality, undoubtedly belong to the court school in Istanbul since there are similar studies in an album made for Murat III in 1575. The Cleveland Dragon drawing, one of the finest of the group, 79 almost certainly came from such an album. Its brilliantly animated design, with the characteristic grey-brown monochromism, and purely decorative quality are typical of these drawings. As already mentioned many of them were probably made as models for tile and pottery painters, textile designers or perhaps bookbinders. Their close relationship with Timurid drawings and book-bindings indicates a possible derivation from the style of Herat, Tabriz, which was conquered by the Ottoman Turks at various times in the early 16th century, serving as an intermediary.

Ottoman painting, however, generally has an entirely different form. Blunt in colour, austere in composition, and entirely Ottoman-Turkish in iconography, the paintings illustrate historical texts of the period, the *Selim-nameh*, the *Sulayman-nameh*, the various books of Festivals (*Sur-* 70 *nameh*, etc.). There are also some that illustrate an extraordinarily important text—a lengthy version of the life of the Prophet *(Siyar-i Nabi)* produced by a Turkish poet for a Mamluk sultan in 14th-century Cairo, but known in an illustrated version only from late 16th-century Istanbul. The paintings of this edition which seems to have been prepared in six volumes for Sultan Murat III in 1594, are in the typical Ottoman court style of large figures in brilliantly coloured costumes, fine, expressive faces, simple landscapes or highly decorative architectural interiors and an original and intensely pious quality that is truly remarkable.

The paintings of the *Sulayman-nameh* are more typical in both iconography (battle and court scenes of the day) and style—compact, densely designed compositions with many human figures. Entire armies fighting in an open landscape or around a city are often represented in one small painting. They are colourful and undoubtedly tell the story they are supposed to tell clearly and directly, but they lack the intensity of feeling or the simplicity of expression that so many of the *Siyar-i Nabi* paintings have. **69**

Ottoman painting has often been regarded as a poor imitation of Persian painting. In fact Persian painting exerted very little influence on the early Ottoman school and none on the court style of the 16th century, which had different aims and followed entirely different principles. While most Safavid Persian painting is not concerned with the real world, but follows a romantic, poetical ideal, illustrating the poems of the past according to long-established pictorial traditions, Turkish painting is intensely and almost exclusively interested in the actually existing world. The history of the day and the actions and events of court and city, the life of the Sultan, his battles and victories, his absolute government are illustrated repeatedly, together with the almost ritualistic audience scenes, and the individual characteristics of the sultan reflected in many portraits. The Persian romantic and poetic subject-matter resulted in a romantic, poetic and sinuous style, while Ottoman court painting is almost harsh by comparison and reflects the rigidity of the centralised power of the Ottoman rulers.

THE TURKISH RUG

The most famous of Ottoman art-forms and that most intimately related to the Turkish spirit is the knotted rug. It came with nomadic Turkish tribes from Central into western Asia, and yet the knotted rug, developed from their primitive fur-imitation floor covering, became the most 'Islamic' of Islamic art-forms. In the use, form and decoration of the rug are embodied most of the fundamental elements of Muslim culture. It reflects the nomadic origin of most of the ruling peoples of the Muslim world; it continues throughout the ages to be a main element of interior decoration being used as floor covering, tent ornament, baldachin and symbol of the royal throne and embodies the most typical of Islamic art-forms, the infinite pattern, in a most perfect way.

Up to the late Timurid period the rug has an abstract repeat pattern of which only part can be seen within the borders, suggesting its continuation beyond that into limitless space, the 'infinite'—such patterns being at all times a symbol of the Muslim concept of the transient quality of all finite forms. Then at the end of the 15th century, the pattern becomes floral (and eventually at the 16th-century Safavid court in Tabriz, pictorial). But at all times—with very rare exceptions in India—the principle of infinite repetition of all pattern elements in all directions is maintained.

Hardly anything is known about rug-weaving centres in Anatolia. Most of their names are trade names, or really 'nick-names' derived from peculiar (often misunderstood) individual elements of rug patterns, or are called after 16th-century European painters who included such rugs in their pictures, or simply places where certain rugs were collected and sold.

73   The 'classical' Turkish rug is the so-called Holbein type, abstract in pattern and restricted in colour palette. The designs are usually based on interconnected staggered rows of polygonal medallions composed of white interlaced

80. 'Bird' Carpet from Turkey, *c.* 1600. 14 ft. 7 in. × 7 ft. 7 in. (4·27 × 2·14 m.). Metropolitan Museum of Art, New York. Ex collection Joseph V. McMullan. These rugs, probably also made in or near Ushak, take their name from the curious resemblance of the continuous leaf motif arranged around a central floral rosette, to small birds. The particular feature of this type of rug is the use of white as a dominant colour.

derived not from abstract linear ornament but from natural bands and highly stylised abstract blue, green or black arabesques on a brick-red ground. This rug is the final product of a long line of tradition that goes back to Seljuk and very likely pre-Islamic Central Asian times.

A fundamental change took place in 16th-century Iran with the introduction of the large-scale medallion pattern developed in Herat (seen in some of Bihzad's paintings). The rugs from Ushak following the Persian concept are **72** designed on the basis of successions of large oval medallions. Those adhering to indigenous tradition have rows of beautifully drawn stars, filled with floral elements or more often abstract arabesques in white and yellow on a deep cobalt blue ground, outlined in white against the magnificent red that distinguishes the classical Anatolian carpet.

Of a very special design are the so-called 'bird-carpets', **80** named after a characteristic floral motif that does indeed resemble a bird. Here again the ancient, abstract concept of a continuous small-scale pattern in the purely Turkish tradition prevails, but almost all the pattern elements are

81. Great Mamluk silk rug from Egypt. 16th century.
Vienna Museum. Following an ancient local tradition of
abstract design, based both on classical and late classical
models, the designers of the Mamluk rugs created patterns of
great originality and imagination. Strictly abstract-geometric in
their basic organisation the only relieving element in these

severe designs is the small repeated floral motif of a papyrus
shrub, a rolled leaf, and a cyprus tree. They are remarkable in
that there is often virtually no division between the border
and the field. Mamluk rugs also have a highly original colour
combination.

floral forms. The peculiar colour scheme of an ivory white
background and deep blues and reds for the pattern elements is unique among Islamic rugs.

74   Egypt was conquered by the Ottoman Turks early in the
16th century. The Mamluks had created a rug form of their
own, independent from any of the major traditions established in Turkey and Persia. Relying largely on ancient,
81   pre-Islamic traditions of textile design, the Mamluk rug
71   weavers developed a kaleidoscopic rug-pattern making use
of classical floor mosaic designs, Coptic textiles and contemporary marble-floor designs that followed ancient
classical tradition. The field of the rug was divided into
small geometric units all of which are equally filled with two
kinds of motifs: a small papyrus shrub, and a rolled leaf.
Secondary decorative elements are what appear to be
highly stylised cypress trees and interlace-band ornaments
and arabesques. Usually organised around a large polygonal or star-shaped central medallion, no part of the rug's
surface is left undecorated, or 'unorganised', that is,
independent of the geometric pattern.

    The colouring of these rugs is as unique as their design.
The ground is deep burgundy red, the main pattern
elements light grass green, the secondary ones light blue.
Only occasionally white and yellow are used. As there is no
colour contrast between field and border hardly any
difference between the two areas exists, although the borders are designed in a more conventional, traditional way,
with successions of small multi-lobal and large oblong
cartouches.

    The Mamluk rug did not survive the Ottoman conquest.

At first Ottoman floral patterns entered into a strange
marriage with the Mamluk-Egyptian concept of unified 74
colour-scheme and general abstraction. But soon the
Ottoman concept entirely transformed the Mamluk rug.
The beautiful wine red remained as a basic ground colour,
but the pattern elements, now floral in design, were bright
white, yellow, blue and green.

Ottoman art shows an entirely original style in every
sphere—the new dome-chamber mosque in architecture,
new floral polychrome decoration in tilework and pottery
and the application of a new, and, in its results, highly
successful canon of colour, composition and iconography
in painting. Although highly decorative and following the
general tendency of Islamic architecture in dissolving the
solidity of building materials and disguising structural
feature by means of magnificently elaborate tile decoration, their architecture has an imposing strength and
masculine quality altogether different from the effeminate
sweetness, floral and arabesque fantasy and colour spectacle
of the contemporary Safavid architecture. The main
achievement in Ottoman architecture is the illusion of a
floating architectural interior with truly architectural
means—through ingenious design and the perfect mastery
of constructional problems. A major feature of Ottoman
art is the play on contrasts—between tectonic qualities and
the dissolution of materials, between realistic forms with
closely rendered details and abstraction in colouristic
effects or in the traditional infinite pattern. In its richness
of invention, excellence of technique and beauty of design,
Ottoman art stands out from Islamic art as a whole.

Safavid Iran

With the Safavids, a Persian dynasty ruled Iran once again. Shah Ismail who ascended the throne in 1502 at the age of fifteen, defeated the Turkomans and Uzbeks alike and united Iran, creating the basis for a new, national culture. He was followed by Shah Tahmasp (1524–76) who moved the capital from Tabriz to Kasvin in 1548 to evade the constant raids of the Ottoman Turks. Safavid culture reached its peak during the reign of Shah Abbas I (1587–1629), who in 1598 moved the capital to Isfahan, in the heart of ancient Persia, where it became the centre of eastern Muslim art and culture for almost two hundred years.

ARCHITECTURE

Almost nothing of early Safavid buildings, of palaces or mosques in Tabriz or Kasvin, has survived. Only descriptions can give us an approximate idea of the lost splendours of Shah Ismail's gardens and Shah Tahmasp's pavilions decorated with tilework and paintings, and filled with rugs and precious objects of all kinds.

75   In Saveh, one major mosque from Shah Ismail's time survives: it was erected in the early 16th century on the traditional court and four-ivan plan with a beautiful prayer hall and dome-chamber. The mihrab, following long tradition, is in carved and painted plaster. The decoration of wall surfaces with painted plaster and glazed brick and tilework, using calligraphic and abstract-linear elements for both inside and outside the dome also follows a tradition that goes back at least three centuries. The building is of a peculiarly archaic nature—especially beside the dazzling splendour of Timurid antecedents and later Safavid monuments in Isfahan.

Safavid architecture is mainly known to us through the 17th-century buildings of Isfahan. When it became the capital, the city was greatly enlarged. A huge palace complex was erected of which only the gate-structure and a few garden pavilions survive. The entire city was re-organised on a grandiose plan. City-planning on a large scale is very rare in the Muslim world and only in a few instances was the usual concept of natural growth, or simple conglomeration of buildings around an important existing structure, abandoned and an all-out effort made to build an entire town according to a plan.

The Maidan-i Shah, a polo-ground designed as part of the royal city complex, is a huge open space surrounded on all sides by screen walls which are decorated with the traditional Seljuk pointed arch-niche motif on two storeys. The square is so enormous that it does not create a feeling of organised space. Only three major building complexes lead on to the Maidan-i Shah: the Ala Kapi, the main gate structure of the Shah's palace that served as grandstand for the emperor and his entourage, the mosque of Shaykh Lütfüllah and the Masjid-i Shah. The Ala Kapi and the Shaykh Lütfüllah face each other across the southern half of the square. The Masjid-i Shah's great gateway takes up a good third of the southern side. Opposite the Masjid-i

Shah, but dwarfed by the vast distance between the two structures, is the main gateway to the bazaar.

The Masjid-i Shah follows Seljuk tradition in all its major elements. The large central court is surrounded by open pointed-niche arcades on two storeys, as in the Maidan, repeating a motif used in the same city in the great Seljuk mosque, and which is also the main feature of the screen wall of the Maidan. In the centre of each side is the traditional ivan-hall, each leading to a domed chamber, a feature already used in the Bibi Khanum in Samarkand in the 14th century. The main ivan on the kibla side is of extraordinary size, its framing portal flanked by tall minarets; the dome chamber is immense and the main dome has a bulbous cupola upon a high drum of monumental proportions. The large rectangular areas between the side ivan-halls and the prayer hall are filled with two open-court madrasahs. The brilliance of the faience coating of the entire surface, dominated by a bright light blue, compensates for the relatively inferior detail. The vast surfaces that must have been covered in a very short time—the mosque was begun in 1616 and completed in 1620—required a simpler technique than the faience mosaic of earlier periods, which was only used for especially important details. The majority of the interior is covered with polychrome painted tiles, usually square. The patterns, all floral abstract, are of brilliant whites and yellows. The total effect of the building is that of a floating world in which all material qualities have been eliminated.

The Masjid-i Shaykh Lütfüllah, built between 1602 and 1618 has an entirely different plan, without court and ivan-halls, a simple, large, square dome chamber being the main feature. Its decorative principle is similar, however, with the interior of the chamber decorated with magnificent coloured faiences, blue and yellow dominating, and the outer surface of the dome decorated with an arabesque design not dissimilar to that of the Shah's mosque. It uses a soft yellow as the main background colour, contrasting with the dazzling blue of the interior. Both domes, that of the Masjid-i Shah and that of Shaykh Lütfüllah are designed on the double dome principle with a low shallow inner shell and a higher elevation on the outside. While Shaykh Lütfüllah's dome is of moderate height and recalls the more restrained Seljuk form, that of the Shah's mosque resembles Timurid domes in its bulbous outline.

PAINTING

Tabriz, seat of Shah Ismail's court and centre of Safavid culture for almost half a century, benefited greatly from painters who were brought to Tabriz by the Shah after he had taken Herat from the Uzbeks in 1510. They brought with them a great many illustrated manuscripts and albums filled with miniatures of the Herat school. It is therefore only natural that the early Tabriz style is very similar.

The true heir to the Herat style was, however, the Uzbek court in Bukhara. The Uzbeks had taken Herat at the beginning of the 16th century and Shaybani Khan, reputedly,

82. **The Masjid-i Shah in Isfahan,** seen from the terrace of the Ala Kapi. Placed at the narrow east end of the huge Maidan-i Shah, (the main square in the centre of Safavid Isfahan, planned and contained within screen walls by order of Shah Abbas in 1611–1612), the Great Mosque of Shah Abbas was erected between 1612 and 1620. The decoration, mainly blue tilework and partly faience mosaic, was, however, not completed before 1630. Possibly it was only at this date that the immense inner

83. **The Masjid-i Shaykh Lütfüllah in Isfahan.** Exterior view. Iran. Early 17th century. This beautifully designed small mosque on the north side of the Maidan-i Shah, opposite the Ala Kapi, the entrance gate to Shah Abbas' palace, is one of the most successful buildings of the Safavid period. It was built by order of Shah Abbas between 1603 and 1618. Only the mihrab in the interior, dated 1028 (1618), is signed by a certain Muhammad Riza ibn Husain. It is not certain whether he was also the architect of the building. The mosque follows a plan totally different from that of the traditional four-ivan court mosque pattern, dispensing altogether with the court and concentrating on a magnificent central domed room.

courtyard with its massive ivan halls was completed. The design of the mosque follows the traditional Seljuk pattern, but adds dome chambers behind the ivan halls and at the sides of the courtyard, a motif that had first been employed in Central Asia in the late 14th century, (the 'Bibi Khanum' in Samarkand). Of immense size and sumptuous decoration, this building epitomises the aspirations of Safavid architects. The principle architect was Ustadh (Master) Abu Ali Akbar al-Isfahani.

took great personal interest in the art of book design, so much so that he seems even to have interfered with Bihzad's own work. Bihzad, the greatest master of the late Herat school must have gone to Bukhara as Ismail would certainly have taken him to Tabriz if he had still been in Herat. He must have returned there and then gone to Tabriz, at a later date, probably shortly before 1521, when Shah Tahmasp decided to reorganise the *Kitab-khane* (the bibliophile academy), making the great Herat master *kitabdar*, or general director.

The Bukhara school continues the Herat style far into the 16th century without any major change. In fact many of its early 16th-century works are difficult to distinguish from those of the Herat workshop. Gradually a certain stiffness of design and a tendency toward stereotyped figures invade the style which eventually becomes highly decorative, brightly coloured and largely unnaturalistic— quite different from the Herat style.

Bukhara painting had, however, a certain sumptuous-ness, successfully elaborate compositions, highly decorative and stylised landscapes and architectural settings, and a magnificence of colour treatment that went far beyond the subtlety and restraint of the Herat school.

Only a few Tabriz painters continued the tradition of realism and it was their work that maintained the vitality of the Tabriz school and brought eventual success.

Mir Sayyid Ali was one of the two masters who accom-panied the Indian emperor Humayun, who spent some years in Tabriz, to Kabul whence they proceeded to India and created the Mughal style (often incorrectly called the Indo-Persian style). He was perhaps one of the finest painters in the realistic tradition in Tabriz. The double-page composition of city life and life in the nomad camp is a

84. Masjid-i Shah, Isfahan. Early 17th century. Detail of the faience decoration showing the extraordinary richness and variety of the decorative motifs and the complexity of vaulting systems largely employed for purely decorative effect.

85. Drawing by Sadiki-beg. *Portrait of a Turkman.* 6¾ × 4⅛ in. (17·2 × 10·5 cm.). Museum of Fine Arts Boston. Sadiki-beg, one of the finest draughtsmen of his time and particularly famous for his portraits, must be accepted as the author of this remarkable pen drawing even though the 'signature' in the lower left hand corner is probably a note of attribution perhaps made at the time. The masterly handling of the wavy outline creating effects of volume and light and shade through varying the thickness of the line, betrays the great artist's hand.

brilliant example of his work. In spite of its mannerism and decorative effects, it is principally based on actual observation of everyday life. His men and women are individuals, almost portraits of real human beings encountered in or around 16th-century Tabriz. There is the same realism in the animals, the landscape, or the innumerable minor details of the paintings. The tents and the houses, the implements of everyday life, the costumes and activities all have a precision and accuracy that reveals close study of the real world. This is an exceptional moment in Persian painting, but it is of great significance. Although it does not last and although the main talents seem to have passed to India, some of the spirit of this painting survives later in the century when the court moves to Kasvin.

Painting in Kasvin continues the Tabriz style at first, not so much the later phase but the earlier, more mannered court style. The realistic tradition of the later Tabriz style is followed in drawing. Although fine drawing was already produced in Tabriz as an independent art-form, it was only in Kasvin that a drawing style developed that was basically independent of painting.

Sadiki-beg, one of many artists of Turkish origin at the Persian court, who later became *kitabdar* of Shah Abbas in Isfahan, was probably the greatest master of the new style of drawing that became a major art-form in Kasvin and greatly inspired the art of drawing in 17th-century Isfahan. He is said to have produced thousands of portrait drawings such as that of a seated Turkoman in the Boston museum. This drawing shows all the stylistic elements of Kasvin— the highly energetic line, varying in thickness to indicate light and shadow and giving volume to the forms it defines, the extraordinary economy of technical means and the almost fierce attention to individual features. Many of these drawings are masterly portraits, often with a critical, almost satirical note.

(Continued on page 161)

83 (right). Painting from a copy of Jami's Haft Aurang *(Seven Thrones)*, copied for the library of Abu'l Fath Sultan Ibrahim Mirza, cousin of Shah Ismail II, between 1556 and 1565 in Meshhed. *Majnun before Layla's Tent.* Size of page: 13½ × 9¼ in. (34·2 × 23·2 cm.). Freer Gallery of Art, Washington. The painting illustrates an episode from the story of Layla and Majnun which was copied in 1565. It is one of the most remarkable paintings of the later Safavid period. The painter, in bringing the Kazvin style to perfection, has broken entirely with the conventions of Persian painting of his time. He has disregarded the generally clearly defined outline of the written surface of the page, and has built up his composition in a most unorthodox way. The fine brushwork, exquisite colour balance, extraordinary realism of detail, and audacity of complex patterns emphasised through the arrangement of the tents and baldachins make it both original and highly successful.

84. **Painting from a copy of Firdusi's Shah-nameh,** 1614. *Bahram Gur killing a lion in China*. Page size: 14¾ × 8 in. 36·4 × 20·5 cm.). Spencer Collection, Public Library, New York. The paintings in this manuscript, modelled on the famous Gulestan *Shah-nameh* (see plate 57) are a conscious attempt to work in the tradition of the Herat School of almost two centuries before. This painting, not based on any one painting, must be a free creation in the early Timurid style.

85 (right). Lacquer-painted bookbinding from a copy of Ali Shir Navai's Divan from Tabriz, Iran. Early 16th century. 9½ × 6 in. (24 × 15 cm.). British Museum, London. Among many fine bookbindings from Tabriz, those in painted lacquer are undoubtedly the most beautiful. The scene here is probably part of a garden reception.

86 (below). Painting by Riza-i Abbasi from Isfahan, Iran. 1630. *Two lovers.* 7⅛ × 4¾ in. (18·1 × 11·9 cm.). Metropolitan Museum of Art, New York. This leading master of the Isfahan school excelled in painting the human figure and, despite stylisation, came close to actual portraiture. This painting of an embracing couple is one of his most delicate and accomplished works.

87. Ceramic bottle from Isfahan, Iran. Early 17th century. Lustre-painted. h. 15 in. (38 cm.). Metropolitan Museum of Art, New York. Much lustreware was made at Shah Abbas' court in Isfahan, reviving an ancient tradition. Animal and floral motifs are typical. The unusual yellow glaze heightens the effect of the lustre-painting.

93. **Emperors and Princes of the House of Timur.** *c.* 1555 (some later additions). Fragment of a painting on cotton. $44\frac{7}{8} \times 38\frac{1}{4}$ in. (114×107 cm.). British Museum, London. Probably the first important painting executed for Humayun in India, this may have been the work of the two Tabriz masters, Mir Sayyid Ali and Abd al-Samad, who came to his court. Unusual both in size and subject-matter, it demonstrates the major features that were to become characteristic of the Mughal school: realism, leading directly to portrait painting, and a most polished technique. True portrait painting is virtually unknown elsewhere in the Muslim World. The composition and almost all the main iconographic features are directly derived from Persian models.

94. **Painting from the Dastani-i Amir Hamza (Hamza-nameh).** India. *c.* 1575. *Assad ibn Kariba attacks the army of Iraj at night.* $27 \times 21\frac{1}{4}$ in. ($68 \cdot 5 \times 54$ cm.). Metropolitan Museum of Art, New York. This is a painting from the first major work of the Mughal school. Originally begun under Humayun in Kabul, the *Hamza-nameh* was made for Akbar. In its paintings the first synthesis was created between Persian and local pre-Mughal Indian styles forming a new, original style that can justly be called Mughal, outstanding in its combination of realism with a sense of composition and pure colour values.

95. Humayun's Tomb, Delhi, India.
1565. This is one of the first buildings on the plan of a central dome chamber with four monumental entrance gates and four corner pavilions. The design is not yet fully worked out—the dome sits too low, the small rotundas (chattris) are ill-related to the main block of the building, and some of the decorative detail, especially the guldastas (a kind of corner finial placed at junctions of walls meeting in an angle) are not very successful. The use of a bulbous 'Timurid' dome (see plate 49) and the combination of white marble with red sandstone in the facing of the building are elements that had a decisive influence on later Mughal architecture.

96. **Painting from a copy of Anwari's Divan,** written in Lahore in 1588. *A Prince riding to Hounds*. 2⅞ × 1¾ in. (7·4 × 4·5 cm.). Fogg Art Museum, Harvard University, Cambridge, Mass. This delightful little painting, probably by Miskin, is a fine example of the early Akbar style illustrations in the minute pocket size codices made for the emperor at his court school in Lahore. While some of them still show a close relationship with Persian and local, pre-Mughal Indian tradition, this painting has achieved the purety of a new style which becomes the basis for all later Mughal painting.

97. **Painting by Abul Hasan.** India. *c.* 1599–1605. *Jahangir holding the portrait of his father, Akbar.* 4½ × 3¼ in. (11·5 × 8·1 cm.). Musée Guimet, Paris. The painting is not dated but in the inscription it is stated that Jahangir was thirty years old when it was painted. Jahangir was born in 1569 and became emperor in 1605. As he is represented as emperor it is likely that the halo and the portrait of Akbar were added at that date. The painting is an exquisite example of official portraiture of the period.

98. **Painting designed by Miskin, painted by Paras, for the Akbar-nameh.** *c.* 1600. *Bullocks dragging siege guns for an attack on the Fort at Ranthambhor, Rajastan, in 1568.* 13 × 8¾ in. (33 × 21·2 cm.). Victoria and Albert Museum, London. This dramatic action painting depicts an actual historical incident during Akbar's campaign in Rajastan. This is in itself remarkable and has parallels only in Ottoman Turkish painting. The scene is represented with great realism combined with an exquisite sense of colour and design.

99. **Painting from the Minto Album, India.** *c.* 1630. *Shah Jahan out riding with his son, Dara Shukoh.* 8¾ × 5½ in. (22·2 × 14 cm.). Victoria and Albert Museum, London. Mughal painting becomes highly ceremonial in this period. The emperor is shown in a static pose; Dara Shukoh is holding, equally immobile, the ceremonial umbrella over his father's head.

100. **Two paintings from a dispersed copy of Sadi's Gulestan,** by Manohar and probably by Ghulam Mirza. India. *c.* 1610. *The Undoing of an ill-natured Vizir* and *A fraudulent pilgrim evicted from Court.* Each 2½ × 3½ in. (6·3 × 8·9 cm.).

Private Collection, U.S.A. Fine examples of the early Jahangir style, these paintings still show Persian influence (landscape and architectural detail) but have new realism and mellowness of colour.

101. **Mughal carpet, India.** Late
16th century. 7 ft. 11½ in. × 5 ft. 1 in.
(2·23 × 1·75 m.). Museum of Fine Arts,
Boston. Mughal India produced a variety
of carpets of great originality, both in
colour and design. The characteristic deep
burgundy red and an intense dark green,
as seen in this rug, are unknown elsewhere
in the Muslim world. The decoration of
the field of this rug with its pictorial
design breaks with the tradition of
abstract, continuous floral patterns
which was standard in carpets before the
Safavid period. It is really more like a
monumental painting in coloured wools
than a carpet in the true sense. The
pictorial rug, first developed in Safavid
Iran, reached its final form in Mughal
India.

102, 103 (detail). **Court coat of a
Mughal prince or emperor,** India.
First half 17th century. 40⅛ × 38¼ in.
(102 × 97 cm.). Victoria and Albert
Museum, London. This coat,
embroidered in polychrome silks upon a
delicate monochrome background, is a
most sumptuous example of Islamic court
dress. The design, consisting of a complex
landscape with animals and birds of many
kinds, follows contemporary landscape
paintings of the Mughal school.

104. Jade cup in form of a gourd, India. 17th century. Inscribed with the name of Shah Jahan and a date corresponding to 1647. l. 6¾ in. (17 cm.). British Museum, London. Jade carving, first fully developed in India during Jahangir's rule, continued into the 17th and 18th centuries at the Mughal court. This is a particularly beautifully carved piece, original in shape and beautifully balanced in design. The piece has special significance as it is both inscribed with the emperor's name and dated.

105. Jade mirror back from India. 18th century. 5¼ × 4½ in. 13·5 × 11·5 cm.). Victoria and Albert Museum, London. The green jade is inlaid with white jade in a continuous cartouche of gold. The white jade inserts are outlined in gold and decorated with a ruby in the centre. Rubies are also placed at the junction of the cartouches. It is typical of the later jades of the Mughals where gold and incrusted juwels have replaced relief carving.

Muhammadi, painter, calligrapher and draughtsman, teacher of Shah Tahmasp and prominent member of the Tabriz academy, excelled equally in painting and drawing. His miniatures became master models for the entire Kasvin school and it is often to him that one accredits the particular qualities of the Kasvin style. In his drawings he follows the earlier Tabriz tradition but adds greater realism.

The Kasvin style, successful for more than half a century, spread to the provincial centres of Iran. Some of these rivalled the capital, particularly in the development of arts and crafts. Among them, Meshhed was very important and here the finest work of the Kasvin style is painted. The copy of Nizami's *Haft Aurang*, now in the Freer Gallery in Washington, is indeed unsurpassed in later 16th-century painting. It is of the highest quality as a manuscript and its miniatures show great finesse and originality.

Shiraz, by contrast, remained independent of the metropolitan style. Even though Tabriz models were sometimes imitated, the Turkoman style was continued into the 16th century, eventually developing into an individual style, which in its best examples, matches that of the capital in quality and imagination. Later on, however, it became stereotyped and purely decorative.

The Kasvin style, that produced its final flourish towards the end of the century, moved to Isfahan. The calligraphic drawing style, developed by Sadiqi-beg was perfected by Riza-i Abbasi, the leading master of the Isfahan school. His paintings follow a similar style with almost impressionistic drawing of hands, costume details, and elaborate coiffures, both of the young ladies and of the effeminate gentlemen of the late Safavid court, and became the models of all later 17th-century painting in Isfahan and the provincial centres.

At the beginning of the 17th century a curious phenomenon occured. A number of manuscripts were illustrated with paintings in the Timurid style of Herat. The Gulestan *Shah-nameh*, made for Baysunghur in 1430, in the possession of Shah Abbas, must have inspired him to order his major painters to create a manuscript that would match the earlier work's particular qualities. The result was the Spencer *Shah-nameh* in New York: the miniatures of this manuscript, painted in 1614 in Isfahan, are nevertheless of great originality in many details, and of a finesse and brilliance of technique that matches the earlier masterpiece. There are also many paintings in this and other manuscripts of about the same period, that follow the Timurid style, demonstrating the ability of the Isfahan painters to revive almost faultlessly a style that had fascinated Muslim artists for more than two hundred years.

THE DECORATIVE ARTS

The Safavid period excelled in all the arts of the book—paper-making, gilding, illumination, calligraphy and bookbinding. To the various forms of stamping, pressing, cutting and gilding of leather, developed in Timurid times, still another brilliant technique was added, lacquer-painting. Although this probably also went back to the

86. **Drawing by Muhammadi,** dated AH 986 (1578 AD). *Life in the Country.* 10¼ × 6¼ in. (26 × 16 cm.). Louvre, Paris. This drawing is an excellent example for the interest in everyday life developed by the masters of the Kazvin school, an element that became of fundamental importance for all later Safavid painting. The drawing is particularly delicate and appealing in its vivid observation of peasants and shepherds in the countryside.

15th century, it was in Tabriz and Kasvin that the first figurative lacquer bindings were created: in their brilliance of colour and variety of design, they rivalled the finest products of the painter's brush.

Equally luxuriant are the patterned silks and brocades of the Safavid period. As little has survived from Timurid times, it is impossible to say whether Safavid textiles go to the credit of Timurid tradition, but it seems from miniatures that the figuratively patterned silks like those from the Tabriz court looms were unknown in Timurid times when gold embroidery seems to have been the main feature. Already in the early 16th century, richly patterned silk brocades seem to have been made for hangings, tent covers, cushions, saddle-cloths, and for garments of the nobles at the Safavid court. They can be seen in many miniatures and some magnificent pieces have survived.

But the most famous textile products of the Safavid period are undoubtedly the large knotted rugs. Persian rugs, abandoning entirely the Turkish tradition of abstract textile design that had dominated rug patterns right throughout the 15th century, are developed on the basis of floral and figurative designs.

The great arabesque rugs of the early Tabriz school, magnificent in their intricate scroll-patterns and strong but

87. **The Ardabil Rug from Tabriz, Persia.** Made by Maksud al-Kashani in 1539–40 for the Shrine of Shaykh Safi in Ardabil. First half 16th century. 36 ft. 6 in. × 17 ft. 6 in. (11·52 × 5·34 m.). Victoria and Albert Museum, London. This is probably the most famous of all Safavid carpets. It is dated and signed and it was made by order of Shah Tahmasp for the Shrine of the family sanctuary in Ardabil. Its sombre colours and elaborate floral design are relieved by the magnificent central medallion that has been rightly compared with the patterns in the domes of Safavid mosques. The reflection of a dome design is emphasised by the appearance of mosque lamps hanging from the central medallion.

88a, b. **Hunting carpet from Kashan (?), Iran.** Woven in coloured silk. 16th century. Size of the complete rug: 22 feet 4 in. × 10 ft. 6 in. (680 × 320 cm.). Österreichisches Museum für angewandte Kunst. Vienna. This elaborate carpet has a richness of figurative detail both in field and border, a sumptuousness of colour and a fine technique that make it the highest achievement in an art form that, after centuries of development along traditional lines of abstract textile design had taken an entirely new turn in Safavid Iran. The rug was clearly designed by one of the leading court painters and many of its numerous figures can be found in the paintings made in Tabriz during the first half of the 16th century.

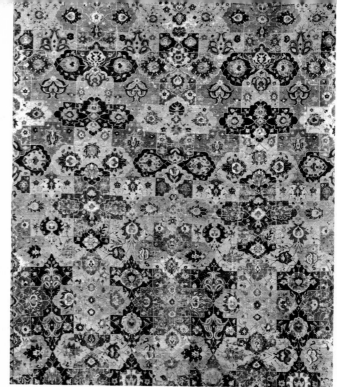

dark colours are still fairly abstract in nature. A few figurative motifs, birds and small animals, are included, but most of the design is based on large-scale systems of superimposed spirals that form an infinite pattern. Central medallions create the illusion of a centralised composition but sections of other medallions in the corners of the field show that they are only part of the composition of staggered rows of enormous stellate forms with cartouches and pendants filled with floral and arabesque designs. The huge rug from the shrine in Ardabil, of 1539, is probably the major work of this type.

It appears that in Tabriz the masters of the *Kitab-khane* began to assume primacy among the creative artists, pushing the weaver into a secondary, craftsman's position. This movement towards the pictorial rug, designed not by textile weavers, but by painters and book-illuminators, leads eventually to a complete change and decadence in rug patterns. Although magnificent in their sumptuous effect, Safavid rugs are actually products of a highly manneristic and decadent era that had entirely lost touch with the strength and simplicity of earlier tradition. Figurative carpets of the type so well represented by the piece in the collection of Prince Sanguszko, clearly illustrate this. Although usually attributed to Kashan, there seems no reasonable doubt that these rugs were made in Kasvin as their figurative patterns seem to have been almost exclusively drawn by the court painters there. The Sanguszko rug is, in fact, no longer a carpet but a monumental painting in coloured wools. The same applies to the large hunting carpets often in silk, like the largest and most elaborate piece in Vienna. Again usually attributed to Kashan, they could equally well have been made in Tabriz and Kasvin. They follow patterns from the two Safavid capitals, their designs being executed by leading painters of the court workshops who again only use the incredibly refined technique of rug weaving to create paintings in wool and silk.

The Caucasus, somewhat remote from the whims of the metropolis, continued an austere and more traditional form of textile design, creating rugs of greater simplicity with stronger design elements. Among them are the formal garden rugs, developing a beautifully balanced and relatively simple pattern of great force, based on a bird's eye view of a Persian garden, with central water courses, lateral canals, trees, flowers and highly stylised pavilions. From here it is only a step towards the more abstract and truly infinite textile pattern such as appears in a carpet which seems to be a unique survivor of its kind. Although closely related to the so-called vase carpets, usually associated with south Persia, it was probably produced in Isfahan. Its field is divided into a continuous pattern of small, geometrical compartments, of different brilliant ground colours, filled with beautifully drawn palmette blossoms of an extraordinary range of colours and shapes.

As in Timurid times the Safavid potter's main achievement lies in immense quantities of polychrome tiles for

89. **Woollen carpet with interpenetrating cartouche design from Iran,** southern school or Isfahan, 17th century. 16 × 9 ft. (4·87 × 2·74 m.). Metropolitan Museum of Art, New York. This rug is technically closely related to the so-called 'vase' carpets that are woven on a double weft and warp structure and it also employs a colour scheme normally found in those carpets. In its particular cartouche design and in its richness of colour it may, however, be the only piece combining the traditions of the north-west and east Persian compartment designs with the floral patterns of the vase carpets which are generally believed to have been made in the south, perhaps in Kerman.

90. **Ceramic plate with a zodiacal design from Iran.** Dated AH 971 (1563–64 AD). Signed by Abd al-Wahid. diam. 16⅛ in. (41 cm.). Staatliche Museen zu Berlin. Persian pottery of the 16th century is rare. Dated pieces like this are almost non-existent. This large plate with a zodiacal design and arabesque patterns in black and blue probably represents an entire school of Safavid ceramic making of which nothing else has survived. It shows particularly well the peculiar way in which the Safavid ceramic painters reacted to the blue and white fashion. The design is practically free of references to Far Eastern motifs.

91. **Wall tile panel with a garden scene from Isfahan,** Iran. *c.* 1630. l. 6 ft. 6 in. (19·8 m.). Metropolitan Museum of Art, New York. The design of this tile panel follows the style established at the Isfahan court school by the leading painter Riza-i Abbasi in the early 17th century. That Riza and his master pupils worked for the ceramic factories is known and a close follower may have painted this garden scene. The inclusion of a European in the painting shows how the European element had become part of the late Safavid court in Isfahan.

92 **Ceramic bottle from Kerman, Iran.** *c.* 1550. h. 12⅝ in. (32 cm.). Museum of Decorative Arts, Berlin. Typical of Safavid pottery of the period, the figurative element plays a predominant part in the decoration of this bottle. The bold contrast between the undecorated white ground and the single energetic figure of a lion-kylin make this piece unusually successful. It also shows that the Far Eastern element, prevalent in all other Safavid design, also entered into pottery decoration.

architectural decoration. Although tile mosaic had passed its peak in the late 15th century, it was still used, especially in early Safavid buildings, soon to be replaced by a less delicate polychrome glazed tile decorated with a section of a given design—a whole panel of tiles making up the complete pattern. This simpler, much cheaper technique was widely employed in Isfahan. Entire surfaces, inside and out, of Shaykh Lütfüllah, Masjid-i Shah, and the Madrasah Madar-i Shah and others, are so covered, creating a dazzling effect of cobalt blue, white and yellow colour and pattern quite unique in Muslim architecture.

90 Of actual pottery, only few early 16th-century types are known, continuing the blue and white fashion. Most known pieces—small plates, bowls, bottles, vases and large dishes—seem to belong to the 17th and even 18th century and only few later 16th-century pieces survive. The so-**60** called Kubachi ware of the 15th century is continued but changed in colour with designs at first largely based on Far Eastern motifs. Eventually Chinese motifs give way to Safavid-Persian iconography. Portrait busts of young men and women, holding flowers, or just gazing out at the beholder follow entirely official Isfahan court painting and the pottery was probably made there in the late 16th–17th centuries. Large numbers of figurative tile panels also repeat subjects and compositions of the court style associat-91 ed with Riza-i Abbasi. The Chinese fashion, although not continued in Kubachi ware, was carried on throughout the Safavid period in the pottery centres. Kerman and Meshhed seem to have been the main centres of fine semi-porcelain production. On brilliant white ground, Chinese motifs such as lion-kylins, dragons, the phoenix and flying

crane are painted in blue, green and yellow. In Meshhed figurative and abstract motifs were mixed, but the deep cobalt blue colour always dominated the design.

The technique of lustre-painting was rediscovered in Safavid times and a great variety of types was created.

Of great charm and interest are the flat-sided bottles created by the Safavid potters, following to some extent ideas from China but endowing them with great originality. These bottles are decorated with low carved and moulded relief on all sides, sometimes with figurative subjects reflecting themes of contemporary painting, but often of an abstract nature, composed of a variety of arabesque motifs. The glazes are brilliant and of intense colours, brown, yellow, green and a combination of purple, rose and white.

Safavid architecture, the last stage of the development of Seljuk forms, was transformed by decoration. The great mosques in Isfahan are entirely in the traditional design but they carry to an ultimate height the Persian ideal of colourful decoration. The dissolution of tectonic qualities and the disguise of structure reaches its final perfection. Safavid art excels in sumptuous forms of decoration as in its treatment of the knotted rug and in silk-weaving. In these and other forms of decorative art the figurative element, highly developed in three great schools of painting, comes to the fore. It is in the realm of figurative painting, which develops a richness and variety unparalleled in Islamic art, that Safavid art makes its most remarkable contribution. The emergence of the individual artist and the creation of a personal style is entirely new.

Islamic Art in India

India had already been partially conquered by the Arabs in the 8th century. This first contact was maintained and eventually in the late 16th century the larger part of the country came under the rule of the Mughal emperors, descendents of the Timurids of Central Asia, and a unified Indian-Islamic culture was created.

The first important phase of Muslim art in India developed during the reign of Mahmud of Ghazna, Afghanistan, (998–1030) who annexed a large part of northwestern India and the Punjab to his large Central Asian empire. With the coming of the Turkish nomads, the Ghuzz, and the Ghorid Sultans to India in the later 12th century, the establishment of slave governors and eventually slave king dynasties at the beginning of the 13th, Muslim art began to become an integral part of Indian art. In 1192 Delhi became the capital of a unified Muslim-Indian empire under Kutb al-din Aibak which, however, did not last very long. The Khalji and Tughlak dynasties ruled the better part of India from the end of the 13th to the beginning of the 15th century. The Delhi sultanate came to an end with the sack of Delhi by Timur in 1399 and after a brief period of intermediary rule of the Sayyids and Lodis, and complete independence of the provinces, the Punjab, the Bengal region, and Jaunpur, which had been taken over after 1480 by the Lodis, India was conquered by the Mughals, descendents of the Timurid Prince Babur at the beginning of the 16th century.

The first period of Mughal rule (1526–40) was brief and troubled, and Humayun, Babur's son, left the government in the hands of Afghan generals while he went into exile to Safavid Tabriz (1540–55). Humayun returned to India in 1555 only to die the year after leaving his still unconsolidated empire to his son Akbar (1555–1605). During the period of Akbar's reign and the reign of his two successors Jahangir and Shah Jahan (1605–58) the Mughal style of Muslim India was developed, surpassing anything done before in India under Muslim rule. In painting especially a new standard of excellence was set and one of the finest schools of Islamic painting created.

ARCHITECTURE

At the beginning, Muslim art in India was totally dominated by Hindu forms and building materials. Temples were converted into mosques or Hindu buildings are dismembered and stone pillar mosques erected from the spoils. Very little of these early buildings and their decoration survives, for the Ghorid Sultans systematically destroyed the Afghan cities of the Ghaznavids in India; and Lahore and many of the early Punjab palaces were destroyed by the Mongols in their invasion of 1241.

The earliest surviving monumental Indian mosque is the *93, 33* Kuwwat al-Islam, built by Kutb al-din Aibak in his fortress of Lalkot near Old Delhi in 1193. The colonnades of a destroyed Jain temple, and building spoils from nearby Hindu temples were used to create an ivan-court mosque. A new façade was erected in front of the Jain temple court,

93. **Kutb Mosque (Quwwat al-Islam), Delhi,** built by Kutb al-din Aibak in his fortress of Lalkot near Old Delhi in 1193. This mosque is the earliest extant monument of Islamic architecture in India and its combination of local, pre-Muslim traditions and imported architectural forms is typical of the earliest period. The mosque is built on the ruins of a Jain temple in front of which a screen wall with a large central pointed archway and smaller, lateral arches was built. The main feature of decoration is the low carved relief.

94. **Mausoleum of Iltutmish, near Delhi,** 1235. Built entirely of stone (the dome has collapsed or was never finished) the small building is particularly remarkable for its simple, precise design, and its elaborate but controlled, low relief decoration.

the principal nave of the temple being used as the centre of the prayer hall, and a mihrab inserted into the end wall. The most important feature of this mosque is a monumental minaret, 240 feet high, built in 1199. The Kutb Manar is a ribbed tower built in five storeys of red stone, decorated with beautifully carved inscriptions and floral bands and four elaborately designed balconies, supported by a richly decorated system of corbels. The mosque façade is decorated with similar low relief stone carving. This monumental stone architecture with finely carved surface decoration, to which inlay of different coloured stones and marbles was added during the rule of the Tughlaks, is the standard form of Islamic architecture in India.

94   Tomb buildings and palaces are the two main forms of architecture besides the mosque. Already in the 13th century a peculiar square or polygonal tomb chamber or mausoleum in stone—usually vaulted with a dome made of cement and rubble—was developed, decorated over its entire surface with delicate highly abstract reliefs. Possibly derived from Central Asian prototypes are the oblique walls in the tomb of Ghyas al-din Tughlak in Tughlakbad built inside a heavily fortified walled complex about 1325. Here also the use of white stone in decorative blind niches and band ornaments in the upper part of the four façades of the free-standing, domed mausoleum anticipates the further development of this feature. In Jaunpur, independent of the central Delhi sultanate for more than a century, only taken over in the later 15th century, a form of monu-

95 mental mosque combined traditions of pre-Islamic Indian fortification and temple designs with a highly original use of domes and high gateways, not dissimilar to the frames of ivan-halls in the Seljuk ivan-hall court mosque. Decorative forms of blind niches, decorative bands dividing the gate façades into three storeys and defining the frames of niches and doorways, derived from 12th-century forms in Delhi, were widely used in these mosques.

    Other buildings, especially tomb monuments made use of the old pavilion form often employing a multiple dome design. Probably the most accomplished of these is Sultan

96 Sher Shah's Mausoleum. A central dome surrounded by smaller, secondary domes was also adopted in the Mausoleum of the Emperor Humayun in Delhi, completed 1572, though substantially altered. The open pillar hall of Sher Shah was replaced by a complex substructure consisting of four monumental gateways, one in the centre of each side of the dome chamber and a pavilion-like polygonal room at each corner, surmounted by a small domed pavilion. The main central dome is raised on a fairly high drum reminiscent of Timurid domes in Central Asia. The entire building is set on a large terrace, that has the effect of a platform with the mausoleum in the centre. The pointed niche arcade motif, traditional in eastern Islamic architecture is used here on the terrace façades of the mausoleum, most noticeably in the double storey design of the corner pavilions. Particularly interesting is the elaborate use of white marble 'inlay' both on the terrace façades in fine linear

95. **Main ivan of the Atala Mosque, Jaunpur, India.** 1408. The enormous height of the ivan hall completely obscures the dome behind it. These high, pylon-like ivan hall structures with massive frames in the form of multiple-story towers and a joining arch, are a typical feature of Jaunpur architecture of this period. In spite of a certain awkwardness of the design and the decorative detail, there is an unquestionable grandeur and monumentality to this architecture.

96. **Mausoleum of Sultan Sher Shah, Sahsaram, India.** 1540–45. This mausoleum is the most important pre-Mughal monument of its type in India. It leads almost directly to the Mughal style proper but retains closer ties with purely Indian tradition than any other Mughal buildings. The mausoleum is built on an octagonal plan in two storeys surmounted by a dome. Both terraces are decorated with *chatris*, Indian-style pavilions. There are seven entrance gates creating the effect of a monumental pavilion. The mausoleum, built in sandstone, is placed upon a granite platform with corner pavilions. The entire complex is built on an island in an artificial lake. There is evidence that the building was originally decorated with paintings and coloured tilework.

97. **View of the Delhi Gate of the Red Fort, Agra.** *c.* 1635.
The major building complex of the period the Agra Fort
combines in its design in an almost perfect way both Hindu and
Muslim traditions in India. The formidable fortification consists
of a wall over a mile (2 km.) long, and standing nearly 70 feet
(21 metres) above the surrounding terrain from which it is separated by a ditch about 33 feet (10 metres) deep. The fort
contains the palaces of the Mughal emperors.

bands of cartouches and on the main building where one
can hardly call it inlay or incrustation. The white stone is so
dominant that it becomes an integral part of the entire
design and this is the first fully developed example of the
'polychrome architecture' characteristic of the entire
Mughal period.

The highest peak of Mughal architecture is reached in
the Taj Mahal at Agra, built by Shah Jahan for his wife
Mumtaz-i Mahal (the Jewel of the Palace) in 1629. This
building, possibly one of the most famous in world architecture, and undoubtedly the most renowned of Muslim
architecture in the East, is built on a plan almost identical
to that of Humayun's tomb. The whole building is placed
upon a platform terrace decorated with a (blind) niche
design. Four tall minarets are added at the corners of this
terrace and the entire complex is enriched by an elaborate
gate construction at the enclosure wall. The most extraordinary feature is its dazzling decoration, far outstripping
that of the tomb of Humayun. The entire building is
covered with white marble inlaid with coloured stones of
all kinds in beautiful abstract and floral patterns, a
technique also employed in the interior especially in the
decoration of the tombs, the screens around them and
large parts of the wall surfaces. The effect is that of a
precious object, not unlike the jewel-encrusted jades and
the enamelled gold cups that Shah Jahan had produced in
his court workshops and that number among the finest in
the Muslim world.

Grille marble work, perhaps most richly developed
in the mausoleum of Itmad al-Daula in Agra, built for
her father in 1622–28 by Nur Jahan, Jahangir's wife, is
also used in the Taj Mahal, just as almost every known
technique of architectural decoration appears there.

The two royal palace cities, Fatehpur Sikri built by
Akbar about 1575, and the great Red Fort in Agra, built
by Shah Jahan almost a century later, combine again the
full variety of building types, architectural design and
especially architectural decoration of their periods. Both
epitomise respectively the aspirations of the early Mughal
empire and Akbar's ideal of a synthesis of all Indian
cultural traditions and the final sumptuous fulfilment of
Islamic culture in India.

Fatehpur Sikri, built near Agra, 1569–72, has a palace
complex consisting of a multitude of pavilions, terraces
mosques and mausolea which are extraordinarily varied in
design and decoration. Both Hindu and Muslim traditions
were freely used and the result was a highly successful
synthesis of a great many different styles and forms.
Individual buildings are placed on a series of interconnected platforms, offered in an almost abstract way without
the aid, or perhaps more correctly from the Mughal point of
view, without the interference of a natural setting. Yet the
decoration is full of the most sensitive reference to natural
forms, flowers in particular. The elevation of the palace
city above the ground upon which it stands (practically as
well as metaphorically) is a very original achievement.

While the palace complex of Fatehpur Sikri is predominantly built of red stone and decorated almost exclusively
in a restrained flat relief carving with abstract linear scroll
work as a main feature, many parts of the Red Fort in Agra
are most sumptuously decorated with polychrome and
elaborate inlay patterns. The tomb of Itmad al-Daula,
Shah Jahan's father-in-law, has already been mentioned.
Its design is relatively simple compared with other con-

98 (left). **View into the entrance courtyard, Fatehpur Sikri,** near Agra. Built by Akbar, 1569–72. This imposing entrance to Fatehpur Sikri shows something of the impressive Mughal style of architecture, incorporating both Hindu and Muslim traditions. The rows of raised bell towers are typical of the general aspect of Indo-Muslim architecture, abounding in raised terraces and pavilions.

99 (right). **The Pearl Mosque, Agra.** The Pearl Mosque was built inside the Red Fort in Agra by order of Shah Jahan in 1648. This view shows the prayer hall from the courtyard. A perfect blending of Indian and Islamic tradition in architecture, especially apparent in the combination of the small *chatris* or Indian-style pavilions with the large bulbous 'Timurid' domes on the prayer hall.

temporary or even earlier structures—a central, square pavilion with a roof entirely in the Hindu tradition on a low one-storey block that seems to serve mainly as substructure for a terrace, with four corner towers, polygonal below, round at the top, surmounted by a modified round dome. The entire building is covered with white marble and inlaid with polychrome stone, both forming abstract and floral patterns. Very fine grille work is used in all the balustrades and in the screens that enclose the ground-floor tomb-chamber. Exceedingly rich inlay also decorates the interior, making the building comparable in richness to the Taj Mahal which it closely resembles. Other parts of the palace complex are less rich in decoration but equally magnificent in the use of white marbles, grille work and relief-carving. Beautiful flowers and floral shrubs are carved into panels on the lower parts of walls; abstract ornamentation also decorates walls and ceilings. The Jahangir Mahal is incredibly rich in its detail and is also remarkable in its predominant use of Hindu forms of construction, largely imitating wooden architecture. An important achievement of the Agra Fort is the complete fusion of Hindu and Muslim elements into a unity.

PAINTING AND DECORATIVE ARTS

Mughal painting begins with the invitation of two leading masters of the Tabriz school to Kabul where Humayun kept his court before he returned to India. Abd al-Samad and Mir Sayyid Ali seem to have been the leaders of the groups of painters assembled by the emperor in the work of probably the most ambitious undertaking of book-production in the Muslim East. The copy of the sumptuous *Dastan-i Amir Hamza*, probably begun in Kabul and completed under Akbar in India, is the largest known Muslim manuscript illustrated with full-page paintings—though only a small number of the original paintings survive, as the manuscript was split up. It took fifteen years to complete and can indeed be called the greatest work of the early Mughal school. Even though reflecting Persian traditions—especially in the architectural settings and decorative elements both in landscape and architecture—these miniatures are already of a decidedly non-Persian style. They are of a realism in detail and an intensity of emotion, both in human figures and in the general composition of groups engaged in various activities, quite unparalleled in Persian painting.

Probably earlier and still closer to the Persian tradition are a number of paintings of which some can be attributed to Abd al-Samad. Extremely delicate in brushwork, small in size and with beautifully painted figures, these paintings provided the Mughal school with models for many similar miniatures showing scenes from the emperor's life. The most remarkable is the so-called 'House of Timur' painting. It is unusually large, anticipating the monumental scale of the *Amir Hamza* manuscript, but with all the delicate qualities of the small painting. Minute attention is given to the landscape, particularly the architectural details of the

garden pavilions. Nevertheless, the human figure is also important, and the subject of the painting—the princes and rulers of the house of Timur—is in itself proof of a growing interest in portraiture. Although very Persian in its general appearance, the beginning of a new art of painting can already be discerned.

The Mughal style develops, however, not only on a Persian basis, but equally strongly under the impact of local, pre-Mughal tradition in India. Some of the greatest painters of the early Mughal school, such as Basawan, were undoubtedly trained in the Hindu tradition. This contact with the local Indian tradition can be observed throughout the history of Mughal painting in a mutual exchange of **39** influence with the local schools in the Rajput hills.

Some of the finest paintings of the Mughal school whose style was developed to perfection during Akbar's reign, are **96** to be found in some small manuscripts of great delicacy. Very fine polished paper is used, margins are often decorated with delicate paintings in gold landscapes with animals and flowers—and an exquisite form of calligraphy is used that, in its balance and grace, matches the perfection of the paintings. The three greatest Mughal emperors, Akbar, *100* Jahangir and Shah Jahan were avid admirers and collectors of Herat manuscripts both of the Baysunghur and of the later school (Bihzad) and it is possible that some small and delicate volumes from Herat, at one time in the Indian emperor's possession, had a decisive influence on the formation of this aspect of Mughal style.

Following the general tendency towards realism in painting, 'historical narrative painting' grew up at this time, a phenomenon otherwise only known from the Ottoman period. Paintings of battle scenes, court life, hunting scenes, intimate representations of the emperor and his harim or his family, and actual portraiture record the real lives of the emperors and their times. Akbar had an *Akbar-nameh* produced, illustrated with a great many **98** paintings of events in the emperor's life, especially his military and political exploits. While many compositions are elaborate, with many animated figures in a landscape, or in a court-hall, there are more intimate paintings of less complex nature with more attention paid to the individuals represented. During Jahangir's reign the art of portrait painting seems to reach its height, even though there are **97,99** the first elements of ceremonial art that eventually dominated the style of Mughal portraiture, removing the image of the emperor from the sphere of everyday life to that of a court ceremonial that places him on an elevated level of symbolic representation. The emperor's head is encircled by a halo and he is shown mainly in profile in a stiff position, almost as an abstraction rather than a real person. Official court scenes, especially the Durbar (the appearance of the emperor at a court reception), became favourite subjects. Eventually in Shah Jahan's time this abstraction and remoteness of the emperor was further emphasised by adding ceremonial symbols, such as the nymbus and the umbrella.

100. **Painting by Hashim in an album made for Shah Jahan.** 15⅜ × 10¼ in. (38·8 × 25·8 cm.). India. *c.* 1635. Portrait of the Mullah Muhammad of Bijapur. Metropolitan Museum of Art, New York. In contrast with the rigid official portraits of the emperor, portraits of nobles of the court or local rulers were often painted in the more lively and informal fashion of the earlier period. This is one of the finest examples of semi-official portraiture of Shah Jahan's time, in which the Mullah's features are most sensitively rendered.

101. **Jade box in mango shape from India.** Mid-17th century. 5½ × 4¼ in. (13·9 × 10·8 cm.). Collection of Alice and Nasli Heeramaneck, New York. Unparalleled in its delicate relief carving, this jade box reflects in its design the marble reliefs of flowers and plants at the Taj Mahal, built about 1635 by the emperor Shah Jahan (see plate 92).

In spite of this stylistic development, realism is always one of the most fundamental forces in Mughal painting, at its strongest in general portrait painting, or in scenes of the intimate lives of the people of the day. It even dominates the 'historical' paintings of later periods and can certainly be observed in battle scenes or scenes of individual combat, or in executions and the like, and it is particularly successful in the great many beautiful animal paintings that become an important feature of Mughal art from Jahangir's time.

A similar realism can be noticed in the floral forms of textile art of the Mughal period. Although again dependent to some degree on Persian models at first, Mughal silk **102, 103** brocades or embroideries, and especially Mughal rugs, are **101** full of realistic pictorial detail. Technically extremely fine, often using silk, the Mughal rugs of Jahangir and Shah Jahan are of great beauty and originality. A luxuriant red is frequently used for the field and a rich polychromy for the floral and figurative designs.

The Mughal emperors were, it appears, especially fond of precious metals, gold with niello and enamel decoration, **105** silver, and precious stones. Among the many exquisite objects that have been preserved, a group of very sensitive

jade carvings stand out. Here again it appears that the Mughals followed their Timurid ancestors as a few Timurid style jade carvings bear the Mughal emperors' names. Of **104** great delicacy of form and with relief decoration of exclusively floral nature, some of the pieces imitate fruit or *101* shells, and some again add animal heads for handles. Still others are encrusted with jewels and gold thread.

The most characteristic element of Indo-Islamic art is probably the fusion of Hindu and Islamic traditions, in contrast to other parts of the Muslim world where the pre-Islamic traditions are usually completely assimilated. The general tendency towards rich decoration, both in architecture and in the decorative arts, finds its counterpart even in painting in the use of strong decorative colours inherited from Hindu tradition and in the elaborate use of gold in later Mughal painting. Mughal painting is one of the most successful applications of Islamic principles to a basically non-Islamic tradition. The development of a realism that goes so far as to include portraiture is unique even within the great variety of pictorial forms in Islam.

Further Reading List

Bibliographies

Creswell, K. A. C. *A Bibliography of the Architecture, Arts and Crafts of Islam.* American University, Cairo, 1961

Pearson, J. D. *Index Islamicus 1906–1955.* Cambridge, 1958

General

Aga-Oglu, Mehmet *Remarks on the Character of Islamic Art.* Art Bulletin, 36, 1954

Brockelmann, Carl *History of the Islamic Peoples*, Routledge and Kegan Paul, 1949; Capricorn Books N.Y., 1960

Burckhart, Titus *The Spirit of Islamic Art.* The Islamic Quarterly, I, 1954

Dimand, M. S. *A Handbook of Muhammadan Art.* 3rd ed. New York Graphic Society, 1958

Kritzeck, James and Bayley, R. Winder (Eds.) *World of Islam.* St Martin's, N.Y. 1960

Lane-Poole, Stanley *The Mohammadan Dynasties*, Paris, 1925

Marçais, Georges *L'Art Musulman.* Paris, 1962

Pinder-Wilson, R. *Islamic Art.* Benn, London, 1957

Pope, A. U. and Ackerman, P. (Eds.) *A Survey of Persian Art.* 6 vols. Index vol. Theodore Besterman, Oxford U.P., 1958

Rice, T. Talbot *The Seljuks in Asia Minor.* Thames and Hudson, 1961

Welch, Stuart *The Art of Mughal India.* Abrams, N.Y., 1964

Architecture and Architectural Decoration

Bateley, Claude *The design development of Indian architecture.* Tiranti, London, 1954

Bell, G. M. L. *Palace and Mosque at Ukhaidir.* Oxford, 1914

Brown, Percy *Indian Architecture* (Islamic Period). Leisure Publications, 1959–64

Creswell, K. A. C. *Early Muslim Architecture.* 2 Vols. Clarendon Press, Oxford, 1932, '42

—, *The Muslim Architecture of Egypt.* Vols. I, II. Oxford U.P., 1959

Erdmann, K. I. *Das Anatolische Karavanseray.* Berlin, 1962

Gabriel, A. *Les Monuments Turcs d'Anatolie.* 2 Vols. Paris, 1934

—, *Turquie Orientale.* 2 Vols. Paris, 1940

Hamilton, R. W. and Grabar, Oleg *Khirbat al-Mafjar.* Oxford U.P., 1959

Hill, Derek and Grabar, Oleg *Islamic Architecture and its decoration, AD 800–1500.* Faber and Faber; Chicago U.P., 1964

Hrbas, Miloš and Knobloch, Edgar *The Art of Central Asia.* Artia, Prague; Paul Hamlyn, 1965

Marçais, Georges *L'Architecture Musulmane d'Occident*, Paris, 1954

Muslim Religious Boards of Central Asia and Kazakhstan (Ed.) *Historical Monuments of Islam in the U.S.S.R.* Tashkent, 1962

Pope, A. U. *Persian Architecture.* Braziller, N. Y., 1965

Wilber, Donald N. *The Architecture of Islamic Iran, the Ilkhanid Period.* Princeton U.P., 1955

—, *The development of mosaic faience in Islamic Architecture in Iran.* Ars Islamica, VI, 1939

Yetkin, S. K. *L'Architecture turc en Turquie*, Paris, 1965

Painting

Arnold, Sir Thomas *Painting in Islam. A Study of the place of pictorial art in Muslim culture.* Clavendon Press, Oxford, 1928

Barrett, Douglas *Persian painting in the fourteenth century.* Faber and Faber, 1952

Binyon, L; Gray, Basil; Wilkinson, J. V. S. *Persian Miniature Painting.* London, 1933

Binyon, L. *The Poems of Nizami described.* The Studio, London, 1928

—, and Wilkinson, J. V. S. *The Shah-Namah of Firdausi*, London, 1931

Buchthal H. *Early Islamic miniatures from Baghdad.* Journal of the Walters Art Gallery, V. 1942

Esin, Emel *Turkish Miniature Painting.* Oxford U.P., 1955; Rutland, Vermont and Tokyo, 1960

Ettinghausen, Richard *Arab Painting.* Skira, 1962

—, *Early Realism in Islamic Art.* Studi orientalistici in onore di Giorgio Levi della Vida, I. Rome, 1956

—, *Painting in the Fatimid Period: a reconstruction.* Ars Islamica, IX, 1942

Ettinghausen, E. and others *Turkey—Ancient Miniatures.* Studio Vista, London-N.Y. Graphic Society, 1961

Guest, G. D. *Shiraz Painting in the 16th century.* Freer Gallery, Oriental Studies No. 4, Washington, 1949

Meredith-Owens, G. M. *Turkish Miniatures.* British Museum, 1963

Rice, D. S. *The Aghani miniatures and religious painting in Islam.* Burlington Magazine, 95, 1953

Wellesz, Emmy *Akbar's Religious Thought as reflected in Mughal Painting.* Hillary House, N.Y., 1952

Ceramics

Baghat, Aly Bey *La Céramique musulmane de l'Egypte.* Musée arabe, Cairo, 1930

Ettinghausen, Richard *Evidence for the identification of Kashan pottery.* Ars Islamica, III, 1936

Frothingham, Alice *Lusterware of Spain.* Hispanic Society of America, New York, 1951

Lane, Arthur *Early Islamic Pottery; Later Islamic Pottery.* Faber and Faber, 1958; 1959

—, *Glazed Relief ware of the 9th century.* Ars Islamica, VI, 1939

—, *Ottoman Pottery of Iznik.* Ars Orientalis, II, 1957

Reiflinger, Gerald *Unglazed relief pottery from Northern Mesopotamia.* Ars Islamica, XV–XVI, 1951

Carpets and Textiles

Bode, Wilhelm and Kühnel, Ernst *Antique Rugs from the Near East.* 4th ed. Heinman Imported Books, N.Y., 1958

Erdmann, Kurt *Oriental Carpets.* Universe Books, N. Y., 1960

Kühnel, Ernst and Bellinger, L. *A Catalogue of Spanish Rugs.* Textile Museum, Washington, 1953

—, *Cairene Rugs and others technically related.* Textile Museum, Washington, 1955

May, Florence L. *Silk Textiles of Spain (8th to 15th centuries).* Hispanic Society of America, N.Y., 1957

Reath, N. A. and Sachs, Eleanor *Persian Textiles.* New Haven, 1937

Carving

Beckwith, John *Caskets from Cordoba.* Victoria and Albert Museum, London, 1960

Cott, P. B. *Siculo-Arabic Ivories.* Princeton U.P., 1939

Erdmann, K. *'Fatimid' Rock Crystals.* Oriental Art, III, 1951

Lamm, Carl Johann *Mittelalterliche Gläser und Steinschnittarbeiten aus dem Nähen Osten.* 2 Vols. Reimer/Vohsen, Berlin, 1929–30

Mayer, L. A. *Islamic Woodcarvers and their works.* Luzac, London, and Kundig, Geneva, 1958

Metalwork

Barrett, Douglas *Islamic metalwork in the British Museum.* London, 1949

Ettinghausen, R. *The Brobinski 'Kettle'.* Gazette des Beaux-Arts, 6e. S., XXIV, 1943

Rice, D. S. *Le Baptistère de St Louis and The Wade Cup.* Editions du Chêne, Paris, 1951; 1955

—, *Studies in Islamic metalwork.* Bulletin of the School of Oriental and African Studies, London University. Vols. XIV, XV, XVII, XXI, 1952, '53, '55, '58

Glossary

Amir. The most common title for an administrative officer in early Islamic times; after the 10th century the title was used more generally by the feudal or semi-feudal overlords.

Caliph. The leader of all Muslims; at the beginning the caliph was both the spiritual and political leader of all 'the faithful'. He loses his power in the 10th century and becomes more a religio-political figurehead. The caliphate of Baghdad lasted until 1258 when the last caliph was murdered by the Mongols; but other caliphs were instated in various parts of the Muslim world long before that date (the Umayyad caliphate of Cordoba, 10th century, was the earliest).

Caravansarayi. A resthouse for the caravans along the main trade routes, built both in Iran and Anatolia in large numbers and on a monumental scale.

Chattri. A pointed umbrella-shaped dome in Indian architecture.

Divan hall. A council chamber.

Ghazi. An organised group of Muhammadans, mainly among Turkish tribes, fighting for the Islamic faith, intent on conversion or else the destruction of infidels.

Guldasta. A pinnacle-like motif which appears in all Indo-Islamic architecture after the 14th century. It is usually used where two walls meet, either in a balustrade or at the juncture of two construction walls.

Hadith. *The Traditions* (traditional sayings of the Prophet Muhammad); not by any means as important as the Koran but of considerable influence for the development of all forms of Islamic thought on almost any subject. As they were recorded verbally for a long time, the 'chain' of transmission is of vital importance in determining the authenticity of a hadith. An entire field of study with various schools grew eventually up around this scrutiny of the 'chain'. Often this was found to be inaccurate and a hadith was discarded as apocryphical. Because this always was likely to happen, the hadith never acquired any absolute authority. This is important as it is only in the hadith that objections against representational art or art in general are attributed to the Prophet.

Hajj, hajji. The pilgrimage, one of the religious duties that any devout Muslim had to fulfil during his lifetime, is called the hajj. The object of the pilgrimage is the Kaaba in Mecca. The pilgrim is called the hajji; this title is very often added to a man's name after he had completed the hajj.

Hariri's 'Makamat'. Al-Hariri's famous book relating the travels and adventures of Abu Zayd.

Hejira (or hijra). The flight of Muhammad from Mecca to Medina in 622 AD. The Muslim era is reckoned from that date.

Imamzadeh. The word actually means 'the son of an imam'. It is, however, used in Iran to signify the burial place or mausoleum of either a local saint or an actual descendant of an imam.

Imam. Religious leader of the community.

Ivan (iwan). The ivan hall, a large vaulted hall open on one narrow side and enclosed by walls on three sides, is one of the main features in Eastern Islamic architecture but also occurs in the West (Syria, Egypt). It becomes a standard feature of the 'Persian', that is really the Seljuk Mosque, where it is placed in the centre of each side of the court. The main ivan, is the one in front of the dome chamber at the kibla wall in the centre of the prayer hall. The earliest uses of this four-ivan plan goes, however, back to Ghaznavid times (Palace of Lashkari Bazaar, Afghanistan).

'Jami al-Tawarikh'. *History of the World*, a monumental work in four volumes, written by Rashid al-din, often copied and illustrated. Many of the scenes are mythological.

Kaaba (Qa'ba). Sacred shrine of Islamic containing the 'black stone' in the middle of the great mosque at Mecca. Literally a square (cubic) edifice.

Kaftan. Long oriental tunic tied at the waist.

Khamsa. Five poems, a group of epic poems by Nizami on mystic, romantic and heroic themes.

Kibla (qibla). The direction towards Mecca; the wall in the mosque that faces Mecca is therefore called the kibla wall; it is always in the kibla wall that the main mihrab of a mosque appears and it is against the kibla wall that the covered prayer hall (often curiously called in western publications 'sanctuary') of the mosque is placed. In the Seljuk mosque, the main ivan and the dome chamber are set against the kibla wall.

Kitab-khaneh. Literally 'house of the book'. Name of the scriptorium at the court in which all arts of the book, from paper making to calligraphy, painting and binding were practised. The head of the Kitab-khaneh is the kitabdar.

Kiosk. A light open pavilion or summer house often supported by pillars.

Kutba. The *Friday Prayer*; it was of political significance as the name of the officially acknowledged ruler was mentioned in it, and, of course, the name of the caliph. To be mentioned in the kutba was equivalent with being 'crowned', a ceremony that did not exist in Islam.

Kylin (Kilin). A mythological creature of composite form appearing on Chinese and Japanese pottery and other Eastern decorative objects.

Madrasah. Actually meaning just school, but it is usually applied to the theological school for orthodoxy. The madrasah becomes one of the main building forms in Islam; its origin is disputed but may well have to be traced to Khurassan where very likely the first madrasahs were instituted by the Nizam al-Mulk, the Grand Vizir of the Seljuks. The form follows very much that of a mosque.

Maidan. Square or plaza.

'Manafi al-Hayawan'. *On the Usefulness of Animals*, a natural science treatise written by Ibn Bakhtishu, one of many scientific or learned treatises chosen for illustration by Persian artists.

Manar (Minaret). Manar means actually 'tower' and is used in this sense, but it more specifically refers to the tower from which the call to prayer was chanted, a practice going back to Umayyad times. The earliest minarets were probably the remnant towers of the Roman temenos of the Umayyad Mosque in Damascus. The more frequently used form is 'minaret' (diminutive of manar).

Maristan. The Persian word for hospital.

Mihrab. The mihrab is a niche, or an indication of a niche in the kibla wall or any other part of a mosque facing Mecca. The origin of the form is complex and not altogether clear; it has certain connections with the 'apse' in the classical basilica and a connection even in its symbolic meaning with late classical palatial architecture is not impossible. Also the mihrab seems at the very beginning have to be connected with a burial place (The Prophet is buried in the mihrab of his mosque in Medina).

Minbar. A kind of pulpit, built both of wood (the earliest one in the Mosque of Sidi Okba in Kairouan, Tunisia, dates from the 9th century) and stone. It consisted always of a flight of steps leading up to a pulpit often covered by a small dome. It was also on the minbar that the governor or ruler took position if he decided on questions of law or general policy.

Mukkarnas (Muqqarnas). A design that has been developed by Islamic architects, possibly from the squinch arch, or independently. It consists of various combinations of three dimensional shapes, among them the plain niche as basic element. The patterns created both in the squinch areas of a dome chamber or in almost any kind of vault (and eventually used in complete freedom from any even tentatively structural connection) are usually referred to as stalactites or honeycomb.

Nameh. Writing, epistle or book.

Nisbah. Part of Arabic name designating family lineage or territorial connection.

Riwaq. An arcade surrounding the central courtyard of the mosque.

Sadi's 'Bustan' and 'Gulestan'. *Orchard* and *Rose Garden*, two of the didactic poems, written by Sheikh Sadi (d. 1292 AD), which were adored by the Persians and often illustrated.

Shah. A Persian title equivalent to a king.

Shiah. The movement in Islam that is supported by the followers of Ali and the belief that only a member of the Prophet's tribe of the Kuraish could rightfully become a successor to Prophet (caliph). The Shiah movement is widespread in Islam and it was not before a later period that it became predominant mainly in Iran and parts of Iraq.

Sultan. This was originally a title which was only used by the main leaders or rulers of the Muslim world; in later periods the title is used by almost any of the innumerable petty princes of the local dynasties both in the East and the West.

Sunna. The movement in Islam that follows the tradition established by the Prophet that the successor to the Prophet should be elected rather than hereditary and any Muslim was eligible rather than just members of the Kuraish, the tribe of Muhammad.

Türbe. A Turkish term for a tomb building or mausoleum.

Vizir. A high state official or minister, sometimes given the authority of a viceroy. Grand vizir—chief minister or administrator of a Muhammadan ruler.

Index

Acknowledgements

Photographs were provided by the following:

Colour: Art Institute of Chicago 10; Bibliothèque Nationale, Paris 27, 31, 32, 58; E. Boudot-Lamotte, Paris 62; British Museum, London 52, 59, 64, 78, 93; Camera Press, London 92; Cleveland Museum of Art, Ohio 6, 44; Damascus Museum 3; J. E. Dayton, London 1, 2, 34; A. Demanega, Innsbruck 24; John Donat, London 51; Fogg Art Museum, Cambridge, Mass. 37, 38, 79, 80, 89, 96, 100; Olga Ford, Leicester 23, 76; Werner Forman, Prague 57; Giraudon, Paris 29; Paul Gotch, Shiraz 46, 47, 75; Gulbenkian Foundation, Lisbon 42, 53, 54; Hermitage Museum, Leningrad 14; Michael Holford, London 15, 60, 65, 71, 85, 97, 98, 99, 102, 103, 104, 105; Prem Chand Jain, Delhi 95; A. F. Kersting, London 21, 25, 26; MAS, Barcelona 11; Francis G. Mayer, New York 69, 84; McGraw-Hill Book Co., New York 4, 7, 8, 9, 16, 20, 30, 40, 61, 68, 72, 73, 74, 81, 82, 86, 87, 88, 90, 91, 94; Erwin Meyer, Vienna 13; Museum of Fine Arts, Boston 101; Österreichische Nationalbibliothek, Vienna 28, 43; Pierpont Morgan Library, New York 35, 36; Van Phillips/Feature-Pix, London 45; Josephine Powell, Rome 33, 48, 49, 50; Réalités, Paris 12; Rex Roberts Studio, Dublin 70; Smithsonian Institution, Freer Gallery of Art, Washington DC 5, 17, 18, 39, 41, 77, 83; Wim Swaan, New York 63; Topkapi Museum, Istanbul 19, 22, 55, 56, 66, 67.
Black and white: Archives Photographiques, Paris 86; Alinari, Florence 31, 32; Lala Aufsberg, Sonthofen im Allgau 13; Roloff Beny, Rome 11, 12, 98; Bildarchiv Foto Marburg 3, 61; Bodleian Library, Oxford 63; E. Boudot-Lamotte, Paris 26, 44, 52, 59, 62, 77, 78; British Museum, London 74; Vincent Brown, Manchester 84; J. E. Dayton, London 6; Cleveland Museum of Art, Ohio 18, 40, 79; Johan Donat, London 16, 34, 35; Fotohaus Hirsch Nordlingen 49; Gulbenkian Foundation, Lisbon 75; Paul Hamlyn Archive 5, 7, 28; S. Harrison, London 10; Hermitage Museum, Leningrad 17, 42, 73; Derek Hill, Letterkenny, Ireland 57; Prem Chand Jain, Delhi 95; A. F. Kersting, London 50; Kunstsammlungen Veste Coburg 33; R. Lakshmi, Delhi 96; MAS,

Barcelona 25a, 25b, 25c, 68, 69; Metropolitan Museum of Art, New York 15, 19, 22, 24, 36, 39, 43, 51, 54, 55, 56, 64, 70, 76, 80, 82, 83, 89, 91, 93, 94, 100; Museum of Fine Arts, Boston 41, 85; Museum of Islamic Art, Cairo 27, 30, 67; National Library, Cairo 71; O. E. Nelson, New York 101; Österreichisches Museum für Angewandte Kunst, Vienna 81, 88a, 88b; Paul Popper, London 1; George Rodger-Magnum Photos 9; Staatliche Museen zu Berlin 4, 29, 46, 90; Walter Steinkopf, Berlin 47, 58; Smithsonian Institution, Freer Gallery of Art, Washington DC 14, 23, 38; Stiftung Preussischer Kulturbesitz, Staatliche Museen, Berlin 92; Suleymaniye Library, Istanbul 53; Topkapi Museum, Istanbul 48, 65, 72; Victoria and Albert Museum, London 8, 37, 66, 87; Roger-Viollet, Paris 20, 21, 45, 60, 97, 99.

Paul Hamlyn Ltd. gratefully acknowledge the permission of professor Creswell and the following publishers to base plans and elevations on illustrations in the publications listed below:

A. Choisy, A. *Histoire de l'Architecture.* Georges Baranger, Paris, 1929

B. Lankaster, Harding *The Antiquities of Jordan.* Lutterworth Press, London, 1959

C. and D. Creswell, K.A.C. *Early Muslim Architecture.* Clarendon Press, Oxford, 1940

E. Creswell, K. A. C. *The Muslim Architecture of Egypt.* Clarendon Press, Oxford, 1952

G. Creswell, K. A. C. *The Mosques of Egypt.* The Survey of Egypt, Giza (Orman), 1949.

H. Torres Balbas, Leopoldo *Arte Nazari* in Ars Hispaniae, IV, Madrid, 1949